STANDING TALL

THE MARVEL OF OUR EXISTENCE IS INCREDIBLE

BY DONNA LANCASTER

To Rebecca & Jim ~
Thanks for being
my friends ~ I miss our
visits ~
Peace & Joy to you
beyond measure ~
Donna

Lancaster Publishing
© 2010 Donna Lancaster

Published 2010
Printed in the United States of America
ISBN 978-0-615-36810-8

STANDING TALL

THE MARVEL OF OUR EXISTENCE IS INCREDIBLE

BY DONNA LANCASTER

Cover and Book Design by
Cowgirls Design, Taos, New Mexico

Lancaster Publishing
Whitney, TX 76692

www.DonnaLancaster.net
donnalancaster@valornet.com

Dedicated to Life

Donna as a freshman at Kansas University, Templin Hall, 1950

CHAPTER 1

Ideal:
A picture in the mind; an illusion.

Donna June Hollingsworth was born on a hot June night in Kiowa, Kansas, in 1932. Hospital deliveries were the exception then not the rule. So, Dr. Hammer and a nurse delivered the baby at the Hollingsworth's home. Ethel's pains, which had started early in the evening, surprised her; the baby was not due for another month. Nevertheless, it was time and nothing would stop its arrival.

The glimpse of the newborn baby was horrifying. The legs were barely an inch long and the knees and lower legs were missing. The tiny, misshapen feet attached to the tiny legs had only four toes each. The little finger was missing from the left hand and the index and middle fingers were grown together. All of this in a package that weighed barely three pounds.

Virgil and Ethel were stunned and shocked. The agonizing and overwhelming pain of seeing their child in such a horribly deformed physical body was devastating. Time stood still. To look at the future was impossible.

They had wanted and planned for a daughter.

But not this one.

I am that daughter.

My name is Donna.

This is my story.

At first they didn't know if I would live. With so many body parts missing, there might be internal problems incompatible with life. Dr. Hammer had offered very little hope that I would ever be able to walk. Anxiety, hopelessness, sadness, guilt, anger, helplessness and fear of the future consumed their thoughts. However there were occasional brief moments of joy because I had a bright smile and happy disposition which eased my parents' anguish.

As the days passed Mother massaged my legs hour after hour, perhaps hoping a miracle would happen. Maybe even the pressure of her hands would stimulate them to grow. Maybe it was desperation that made her do it, maybe hopelessness, maybe guilt. There is no way of knowing. As acceptance replaced grief, one thing became certain. I, as her daughter, Donna, would be treated and cared for as any other "normal" child. My differences would never be mentioned or discussed. With that decision, the whole family operated as though they were blind to my handicap.

At the end of two months, I weighed five and a quarter pounds and measured seven and a half inches. By the time four months rolled around I had grown to a happy, healthy handful at eight and three-quarter pounds and ten and a half inches long. Concluding that I was a survivor, Dr. Hammer suggested that Mother and Daddy take me to Research Hospital in Kansas City for consultations. He said that the orthopedic specialists there might have a solution for my physical deformities.

It was 400 miles from Kiowa to Kansas City. In 1932 there were no freeways or toll roads. Some of the roads were not even paved. A neighbor, Anna, volunteered to keep my brothers, Jack and Delbert, so they wouldn't miss three days of school. Daddy serviced his gasoline delivery truck for the trip. Reaching for some hope, yet afraid of not finding any answers, we headed for Kansas City.

After x-rays and examinations, the orthopedic specialists confirmed that there were not enough bones in the right places to enable me to walk. The only possible solution would involve a series of operations grafting bones from Jack and Delbert into my legs. This could provide the necessary bones to support walking.

Mother and Daddy had many questions. Could I live through these long and involved operations? Would the bones taken from Jack and Delbert harm them in any way? Could any guarantee be given that the grafted bones would grow properly? How many operations would they have to perform? How long would I be in the hospital? And the big question: how much would it cost?

The doctors gave only vague answers. Absolute certainty was impossible. It would be an experiment. No promises. It was a tough decision. Mother sensed that my bright, brown eyes, dimpled smile and sunny disposition were bringing joy to the family. She could see a light and sparkle in me much more valuable than short, abnormal legs and an inability to walk. She needed to nurture this light and allow it to develop.

With her jaw set firmly, Mother quietly answered the doctors, "No, we'll wait and see how Donna adjusts to her handicap. Later on she can make her own decision." A thread of hope had been dangled in front of her and she had courageously refused to grab it.

Having made the decision, Mother and Daddy gathered me in their arms and headed back home to Kiowa. During the return trip, they made a commitment, which they kept throughout their lives. They resolved to do everything possible, regardless of their own pain and overwhelming difficulties, to help me construct a self-sufficient life. Every decision would be based on one simple question, "What is best for Donna?" This commitment was to be tested many, many times.

CHAPTER 2

"What is" is reality.
"What ought to be" is illusion.

Mother and Daddy had moved to Kiowa three years before. Although the Depression was in full swing, Virgil had a job with Sinclair Oil Company to deliver gasoline to wheat farmers in the area. Ethel was responsible for raising their two sons, Jack and Delbert, who were six and eight years old when I was born.

Life was simple, but not easy for my family in the early 1930s. Daddy had always worked hard and felt a tremendous responsibility to provide for his family. It was not popular for women to work outside the home so one salary provided all the basics. Mother had taught school for two years before she married, but with Jack and Delbert, and now a child that required special attention, working out of the home was never even discussed.

Soon after the trip to Kansas City, Mother and Daddy watched as I pulled myself along the floor with my arms. One day Mother found me up on all fours like a puppy. She watched with apprehension as I began to climb and crawl over everything; chairs, couches and beds. The instinct to reach out and help me or stop me was powerful. She stifled her impulse to scream, "Stop, you can't do that! Watch out! You'll fall and hurt yourself!" She had made the decision on the way home from Kansas City to do whatever was best for me. In order to do that, she had to control her own instincts and impulses. As I climbed and crawled over everything in the house, Mother remained restrained and silent. She was probably not aware of it, but the greatest gift she could and did give to me was to let me take charge of my own development and progress.

Acceptance did not come overnight. Gradually Mother learned to live a day at a time, without feeling guilty for my handicap or afraid for my future. She found my bright mind and happy spirit delightful and entertaining. Love replaced fear and guilt. It was not a self-seeking possessive love, but a real concern that I would have every opportunity to be me. Yes, it would have been easier if I had been so-called "normal." But that was not the situation. She didn't like it, but not liking it wouldn't change it. Hopelessness and her troubled and heavy heart gradually disappeared. Both Mother and Daddy bravely accepted the hand that Fate had dealt them.

Mother had just finished hanging the clothes on the line one spring day when I was about 11 months old. As she stepped through the door, carrying the empty basket, she suddenly stopped in disbelief. For a moment, she was transfixed. Shock, then amazement, swept over her. I was moving toward her, WALKING! She dropped the basket, scooped me into her arms and ran next door shouting to our neighbor, Anna.

"Donna can walk! Donna can walk! The doctors were wrong! She can walk!"

Up to this point Mother and Daddy could not imagine a life for me without a wheelchair or someone to carry me. They worried that my future would be one of constant dependence. They would take care of me as long as they were able, but what about the time when they could not? How would I dress myself, go to the bathroom and what about school? To them, this miracle of walking was a huge step toward freedom and self-sufficiency. The whole family was ecstatic. However, they knew it would be inconvenient and frustrating to be only half as tall as everyone else. But their outward determination became an inner resolve. They would never see me as having any limitations. I wasn't handicapped or limited. I was just put together a little differently.

Gradually, they became accustomed to my method of walking or running:

wobbling like a duck on my tiny feet. They spent many hours looking for me. I was either in the cabinets, under the bed or other pieces of furniture, in the clothes basket, tucked neatly into a hole in a tree, or any of a hundred other places small and interesting to this curious child.

Mother didn't stop me when I wanted to go outside and play with the other kids in the neighborhood. Nor did she hesitate when it was time to march me off to kindergarten. She knew some kids would stare, make fun of me and call me hurtful and ugly names – but again and again, she remembered her commitment: "What is best for Donna?"

She knew that it was best for me to face the world alone and learn how to handle whatever situations came my way. Curious children were sometimes rude and cruel. Some called me "Wadley Duck." Others asked, "Why are you so little?" I patiently explained to them: "God made your legs long and He made mine short. That's all there is to it." This usually satisfied their curiosity and we all moved on to fun and games.

Jimmy, who lived across the street, and I were sitting on our front steps one morning. Jimmy, also four years old, asked me, "How come you're not tall like I am?"

Glancing at my short legs, I replied, perhaps prophetically, "I'm not old enough, yet. When I grow up, I'll be tall." Grown-ups were more self-conscious than children and were easily embarrassed. At times, when walking down the street, a child would point to me and say in a loud, clear voice which could be heard for three blocks, "Look Mommy. Look at the little girl. She walks funny." The mother was so embarrassed. She would try to shut the kid up and avoid eye contact with me. I would try to catch the mother's eye and send her a silent message which said, "Don't be cross with him. I understand and it's okay."

Many other people, however, were kind and loving to me. Gus, the mailman, placed me gently into his mailbag for the trip around the block. My head was barely visible above the packages and letters. I felt like a "Special Delivery" package and knew of no one else who ever had this wonderful experience.

Mother and Daddy treated me as they would any normal child. When I wanted a pair of roller skates, Daddy bought the smallest size he could find and adjusted them to fit my tiny feet. He buckled them around my crooked shoes and let me go. I bragged to my friends, "I can skate under the kitchen table. I bet you can't do that!" Of course, I fell many times, but fortunately I didn't have far to fall. With practice I soon made the linoleum floors my private skating rink. When Mother had tolerated this indoor skating rink project as long as she could, she deposited me outside to skate on the broken sidewalks! Roller skating in the house was no longer permitted. I would just have to learn to handle the cracks and rough spots as best I could. This was the "not open for discussion" position she took on every learning issue.

On my seventh Christmas, Santa Claus brought me a tricycle. I knew who Santa was, but Daddy was having so much fun, I didn't want to spoil it for him. He watched with fascination as I crawled up to the seat and tried the pedals. My feet could not follow the pedals all the way around, so I pushed hard with one foot and waited for the other pedal to come around so I could push it with the other foot. Riding a tricycle soon became easy and I found the speed exhilarating. The basket on the front was just the right size for books or a loaf of bread. My friends had moved up to bicycles, but for now, the tricycle was all I could handle. The bicycle would come later.

Frank and Anna were neighbors in Kiowa and close friends of our family. Daddy had admitted to Frank early in Mother's pregnancy that he felt something was terribly wrong. Anna, a nurse, gave Mother comfort and solace during the extremely sad and painful days after my birth. We hadn't seen these dear friends for many years. We were living in South Haven by now and I was eight or nine years old when Frank came by to see us.

Supper was almost on the table when Frank stepped into the kitchen. I looked up and started to say, "Hi."

At the same moment, he glanced down at me and said, "Hi, midget."

My insides crumbled. A huge lump arose in my throat and I could hardly breathe. I ran out the back door before anyone could see me crying. I climbed up to the second branch of my favorite tree. I sat in its protective branches for a long time, feeling so hurt and injured. The pain was almost unbearable. "I'm not a midget," I sobbed. "Others must think I'm different, but I'm not." With intense conviction and determination I vowed that no one would ever, ever hurt my feelings again.

Decisions made singly and with great intensity are very powerful. I did not know the mechanics of that power when I made that decision. But now, 70 years later I understand and am happy to report that I don't get my feelings hurt. What an absolutely wonderful gift Frank gave me that day. That pivotal moment in my favorite tree saved me tons of tears and heartache. It freed me of taking everything personally and removed any tendency to play the victim role.

Something had been cut loose inside of me. My energy seemed different. I couldn't wait to join in all the neighborhood games. In hopscotch, I couldn't jump far enough to miss the lines. Who cared? I most certainly didn't! When I played jacks, it was awkward and almost impossible to hold the jacks in my left hand. Who cared? Not I! Hide and seek was a bit easier because I could squeeze into hundreds of small spaces that were impossible for others. I could hide under the porch, in the neighbor's doghouse or in the washing machine. My friends could not find me. Drop the handkerchief was difficult because I couldn't run very fast with my short legs. These wonderful, thoughtful playmates chased me more slowly when I dropped the handkerchief behind them.

Did I feel lonely and isolated? No. Did I feel rejected? No. I became a part of whatever was taking place and with very little encouragement, took charge of whatever was going on.

My friends and I designed a baseball diamond in our backyard. The elm tree was first base; the trash barrel, second; and the corner of the garage was third. The neighbor's strawberry patch was out of bounds. I was catcher and team captain. When it came time for me to bat, the pitcher tried to throw the ball somewhere between the shoulders and knees. Since I didn't have any knees, I usually made it to first base on walks.

The mid 1930s were happy times. I had many friends. School was enjoyable and I made good grades. Mother and Daddy never put me down or made me feel ugly, rejected or different. When my third grade class scheduled a group swimming party, Mother made me a tiny bathing suit. She never conveyed to me any concern that my short legs and crooked feet would be exposed for everyone to see. They did everything they could to help me feel good about myself. Jack and Delbert were supportive as well. Six and eight years older, they were never embarrassed or ashamed to take me with them. Well, that is not exactly true. All three of us went to the Saturday afternoon movie. One Saturday, the movie was about a plane crash. I couldn't keep from crying. On the way home, both Jack and Delbert told me they would never take me to the movie again unless I promised that I would not cry in the movie. I did just that.

However, the late 1930s proved difficult for our family. Because of my father's position as a "trouble-shooter" for the oil company, we moved often. In 1935 we moved from Kiowa, Kansas, to Medicine Lodge. Then a few months later we moved on to Kingman and two years later to Wellington. In 1940 we made our final move to South Haven. Mother scrubbed down each house we lived in so our environment was neat and clean. She was a master at creating a pleasant environment. I never went hungry or felt deprived. Mother made our clothes. We never had a "babysitter." I don't remember ever eating a meal out. We didn't have television, of course, but we played all kinds of games in the evenings. I never heard Mother or Daddy argue or have a cross word about anything. Certainly Mother and Daddy had anxieties when I marched off to new schools. They couldn't live these experiences for me. However, Mother faithfully had freshly baked cookies for the three of us when we got home from school.

CHAPTER 3

Be grateful for pain.

South Haven, Kansas, was a good final move for us. Mother and Daddy had been raised here. Their parents were farmers and Jack and Delbert usually spent summers on their farms. A Derby service station lease was available on the main street, so Daddy entered the gasoline business for himself.

It was rainy and cold that February day when Daddy took over the station. Our living quarters were part of the whole building. True to Mother's nature, within days the cramped quarters were clean and livable. The boys slept on a roll-a-way bed and I slept on the couch in the tiny living room.

The driveway of the station was muddy from the rain. Two tall gasoline pumps (which held ten gallons each) were filled by hand pumping fuel into the glass cylinder which delivered the fuel to a car by gravity flow for eight cents a gallon. Daddy was an intelligent and optimistic businessman and we were in the middle of the finest wheat land in Kansas. The gasoline business could be very profitable.

Then the war began.

On December 4, 1941, an accident happened to me that kept me grounded for seven long weeks. The trapeze rings on the school playground were loads of fun. My cousin Sarah had to lift me up to the rings because I was too short to reach them. However, once I was up I swung like a monkey from limb to limb. This day my hands suddenly started to slip.

"Sarah, help me! I'm slipping!" I screamed. Sarah couldn't catch me before I fell with a thud to the ground. I didn't feel any pain so I didn't think I was hurt. But I couldn't stand up. The right leg had an ugly bend to it.

"Donna's hurt!" Sarah yelled. "Hurry! Someone find Miss Patterson." The fourth grade teacher, Miss Patterson, ran like a sprinter to the scene of the accident. She carefully picked me up and gently carried me to her car and laid me on the back seat. There were no tears, but I could hardly keep from throwing up. Someone called Mother to come to the doctor's office.

The x-rays confirmed that my leg was broken just above the ankle. The doctor gave me an anesthetic, set the break and applied a cast. Usually when a cast is applied to a broken bone, it is necessary to include one joint above the break to ensure complete immobility. Since I had no such joint, the doctor insisted I remain as motionless as possible for the next several weeks. Tough duty for this one.

So, there I was on the couch by the radio on December 7, 1941.

Even though I was only nine years old, I knew that this announcement by President Roosevelt would have a dramatic impact on my family. My brother Jack was 19 and in his second year at the University of Kansas. He knew he would be drafted, so he enlisted in the Army Air Corps. He had wanted to be a pilot, but the Air Corps had different plans for this highly intelligent young man. They trained him as a navigator. When he miraculously returned from his 35 missions from England, he became an Air Corps instructor. When Delbert was old enough, he also joined the Army Air Corps. He missed being a pilot by a few months. His happy-go-lucky nature and winning personality covered up his disappointment.

It seemed that everything was rationed: shoes, gasoline, even groceries. Keeping me in shoes was a problem. My right foot was smaller than the left one. When I walked, the right foot twisted, so the right shoe wore thin very quickly. The kind people in the small town with a population of 400 gave Mother their shoe stamps for me. Gasoline rationing had requirements. For every gallon of gasoline Daddy sold, he had to have a stamp for it. Daddy always had a few extra gasoline stamps and he gave them to traveling soldiers going home or going back to their base. Daddy felt if his sons were on the road and needed gasoline, he hoped that someone along the way would help them. After supper we sat around the kitchen table and licked gasoline stamps and put them in the books required by the government.

Around the house Mother assigned me chores. I had to keep my room clean and neat, do the dishes, set the table and carry out the trash. She tried to maintain a delicate balance between discipline and guidance without which I could become a spoiled and obnoxious monster.

After a supper of greasy fried chicken, mashed potatoes and messy gravy, it was my turn to do the dishes.

"Donna, it's time to do the dishes," Mother directed one evening.

"I'm busy!" I echoed from the back bedroom.

"The dishes are to be done *now!*" she insisted.

I slowly inched my way into the kitchen, placed my stool in front of the sink and sullenly crawled up on it. Still pouting and belligerent, I whined that the water was too hot and the dishes were greasy and messy.

Suddenly Mother jerked me off the stool, slapped me across the face and said, angrily, "I'm tired of fooling with you. I'll do the dishes myself!"

Stunned, I couldn't believe Mother had slapped me. I had never seen her angry or upset. At that moment, I would have gladly washed a roomful of dishes. I can only imagine Mother's remorse at her outburst. "Have I gone too far? What possessed me to be so angry? What a terrible way to treat Donna." These self-condemning thoughts surely tormented her.

But time proved that this choice of discipline was priceless and right on schedule. I needed to learn to accept responsibilities with cheerful good humor. Whining and complaining would not be tolerated. This lesson has served me well from that day until now. I have signs posted around my house: NO WHINING ALLOWED!

Designing clothes for me required some creative imagination. From the hips up I was normal for my age. During the early years, Mother made me sundresses or smocks with matching panties, always using bright, happy colors. Reflecting her acceptance of my unusual physical appearance, she made no effort to cover up neither my short legs (which had no lower legs, knees or hip joints) nor my tiny crooked feet. Shoes that laced up were easier to walk in than slippers. There was barely an inch between the top of my shoes and my designer panties. At age three, it was okay for the panties to show. Everyone thought it was cute. At age 11, it was embarrassing!

At school I overheard a cutting remark by one of the boys.

"I can see Donna's panties," he giggled.

I wanted to slap the sleazy smirk off his face as hard as I could. In dresses my panties showed, or the dress nearly reached the ground. I started wearing slacks most of the time. I was more comfortable when I knew my bottom was covered.

"Riding a tricycle to school is silly," I thought. "All of the other kids have bicycles. What I really need is a bicycle." Of course there was no way I could ride a bicycle. Without knees and very short legs, it was mechanically impossible. However, I had dreamed three different times that I was riding a bicycle. Today I'm not a true believer in dreams. They leave a lot that I question. However, at 12, I was totally convinced that these dreams came straight from the Source (whatever that was) and were prophetic enough that I bought the idea. There was no doubt in my mind. I knew I could ride a bicycle!

Finally, weary of my begging, my parents relented. Daddy found a second-hand, 16-inch girls' bicycle for $15. A local mechanic moved the seat back four inches so it wouldn't jab me in my back while I pedaled.

I straddled the bicycle, put a foot on the pedal, then the other foot on the other pedal and fell down. Time after time I fell, climbed back on, only to fall again. The gravel scraped my arms and legs. The concrete skinned my face and hands. I was bloody and bruised.

Finally, after three days of this physical beating the bike and I managed to stay upright for a distance of 30 feet.

"I'm riding it! I'm riding it!" I screamed at the top of my voice. I felt like I had just earned an Olympic Gold Medal!

The bike tilted from side to side a bit as I pedaled, which compensated for the missing knees. It didn't take long for my skill to improve. The bike and I were inseparable. Off we went to school, to the post office, to the grocery store and around the section, which was a four-mile trip. I couldn't have been happier.

Mother's challenge had been greater than mine. She thought it impossible for me to ride the bike. She had to force herself to keep her mouth shut. Her impulse was to run outside and scream, "Stop it! Stop it! Don't do this to yourself. There is no way you can do it." With tremendous courage and restraint she watched from the living room window, tears streaming down her face as I took this bloody beating. She couldn't tell me that it was impossible. Impossible, against all odds I had learned to walk. She had to let me find out for myself whether I could ride the bike or not. She could not influence me to give up just because it was so painful for her to watch me. To see me ride all over the countryside was her victory as well as mine!

May Hollingsworth, Daddy's cousin, lived a block down the street. She had never married and had taken care of her father, Dr. Hollingsworth, the town's only physician, until he died in 1945. Her life seemed drab and lonely. The family felt obligated to visit her occasionally in her dark and cluttered parlor.

She surprised the whole family when she offered to give me her piano. With only two functional fingers on the left hand and legs that couldn't reach the pedals, it seemed a questionable gift.

The beautiful, black Kimball upright was moved into our tiny living room. Daddy designed an extension which clamped onto the piano pedal with wing nuts. The local mechanic built it. Virginia Gile, the school's music teacher, started giving me piano lessons. I enjoyed the tedious etudes and the boring exercises. If all of this nonsense was necessary before I could play a harmonious song, so be it. I really wanted to learn to read music and learn to play a familiar tune or a snazzy song.

So, for 50 cents each, we started the lessons. At first, the monotonous scales drove the family nuts. The two fingers on the left hand had to work overtime to pick up all the notes. I missed a few, but no one seemed to notice. Before long the notes began to sound like real music. I could enthusiastically play "The Happy Farmer," a work by Robert Schumann, by the way. A love for music was emerging, which enriched my whole life. By the time I was in high school, I had developed enough skill to accompany the various musical groups at school and church. Daddy had another pedal made so I could leave one at school. Miss Gile taught me with patience and skill. At school, she taught all of us to identify each of the various instruments in the orchestra. We could pick out the violins, the horns, the woodwinds and the percussion instruments easily. We listened to the great composers: Beethoven, Bach and Mozart. She was also the focus of some rather juicy gossip. In the early 1940s female teachers were not allowed to marry. Sounds ridiculous now, doesn't it? However, she had fallen in love with Charlie, the county extension agent and they were secretly married. We all thought this was highly romantic. Of course everyone speculated that she was pregnant. The word pregnant was not used, except in a whisper. Instead, we said, "in a family way." If the School Board had known she was married, she would have been fired immediately. Regardless, she made a significant contribution to my love of music.

The index and middle fingers of my left hand were grown together when I was born. When I was 11, Mother took me to Wesley Hospital in Wichita. Saturday morning at Wesley, Dr. Bense, a highly skilled orthopedic surgeon, counseled with parents whose children had special physical problems. His tall, burly appearance was a bit scary, but his heart was pure gold. He suggested that my fingers should be surgically separated so they could be more functional. A surgery date was set. I was to stay in the hospital, a 45-mile drive from home, for several days. Mother was present for the surgery, but I was alone during the night and most of the day. I begged to go home the first night after surgery.

Although it was painful and heartbreaking for them, they remained steadfast. I would just have to get over it, alone.

The children's section on the fifth floor was cheerful, despite the abnormalities with which each one there lived. The nurses and other workers were kind and thoughtful. For instance, I had a small gold ring, which I wore on the third finger of my right hand. Washing my hand under the running water while the other one was bandaged, the ring slipped from my finger and disappeared down the drain. In tears, I ran and told a nurse what had happened. The nurse called a maintenance man, who came quickly and removed the gooseneck pipe from the sink. There lay the ring in all the gook and grime. This was an outstanding act of kindness for my behalf.

Mother was at the hospital on the morning I was to be discharged. When Dr. Bense came for his daily rounds, she asked him, "Is there anything that can help Donna's legs work better?"

"Yes," he answered, with very little enthusiasm. "We can amputate her feet and fit her with artificial legs."

My eyes popped wide open. "Amputate? You've got to be kidding! Never! How could I ride my bicycle?"

In his experience, artificial limbs were customized to fit over stumps that were missing part of a leg. My feet would not fit in the "socket" that encased this stump. He wholeheartedly agreed with my decision. He had worked with enough children to know how well they could adapt to the world in which they lived. He respected the incredible power of the human spirit. I was no exception.

Separating the fingers helped somewhat, but it didn't give me two functional fingers instead of one. Perhaps if physical therapy had been available at that time, the results would have been different. But the middle finger remained useless because the muscles had atrophied. The index finger was limited, but I could type and play the piano easier. My hand did look better, cosmetically. Later on I could wear gloves by removing the fifth finger of the glove and shortening the first two fingers. Alas, custom made gloves!

Sarah, my cousin who watched me drop from the trapeze rings and break my leg, was two-and-a-half years older than I. Neither of us had sisters, so we were very close. She was planning to be a medical technician although she knew very little about it. To me, this sounded like it might be interesting, fun and impressive. I took courses in high school that would prepare me for this career. This schedule included biology, chemistry and math, which didn't leave any hours open to take the dull home economics courses all the other girls in my class were taking. The one course that fascinated me was aeronautics. Intrigued with aviation, I wanted to know how an airplane could fly. This later proved to be worthwhile when I started taking flying lessons.

Most of my courses were difficult and challenging. Therefore, in my freshman year, I wanted an easy course to balance out my heavy schedule. My best friend and classmate, Lucille, had told me that typing was a "snap" course. That was exactly what I needed, a snap course. Little did I realize it would be one of my most challenging classes.

The typing teacher, Miss Stevenson, was a bit befuddled. She was young, obese and had very little imagination. She had never had a typing student with only two fingers and a thumb on their left hand.

She finally confessed, "Donna, I don't know how to help you. You'll have to work out your own system."

Through trial and error, I discovered I could use the left thumb for the keys normally hit by the left forefinger and middle finger. This meant that the thumb would be responsible for nine keys – e, r, t, d, f, g, c, v, b. The right thumb would do all the work on the spacebar. It took a lot of practice, but this technique worked very well and I gained dexterity in my fingers. I could spin out 50 words a minute with reasonable accuracy on the large Royal typewriter. Miss Stevenson happily gave me a "B" in typing. This wonderful course turned out to be invaluable from 1946 until this day. Here I am typing these words into the computer that will shape this story. It reminds me to be thankful for this hard-headed and stubborn little freshman girl and her determination to walk through challenging situations. It has paid off in hundreds of ways.

The county's telephone office had three operators, one for each eight-hour shift, but they needed a part-time relief operator. Since I was only a junior in high school, I could be on duty only nights and weekends, but that seemed to work for the other operators, so despite my age, they hired me.

The phone area had approximately 300 customers. Each had a number, such as "42" or "57F15." The number of each customer was displayed on a large switchboard, with a hole below the number and a small metal piece that dropped down, indicating an in-coming call on that line. A row of 20 or more plugs fit into the holes and stretched in front of this big board, arranged in pairs. When the metal dropped down, a plug was inserted into the hole, a key opened the line and the operator said, "Number please." Then the second plug was inserted in the number requested. Most callers didn't know the phone number, so they asked for "Ted Jones" or "Bill Smith." With only 300 numbers, it didn't take me long to memorize everyone's phone number. Three long distance lines connected the South Haven area to the outer world. The job was fun and an interesting way to get to know everyone in the calling area. Besides, it paid 40 cents an hour.

I had a reason for wanting to make some money. I had spotted a beautiful new portable Smith Corona typewriter for $92 at the Wellington office supply store. I would be entering college soon and a typewriter would be necessary. Mother and Daddy didn't offer to pay for it. My usual attitude of "I'll do it myself" took over and I did just that. It took 230 hours of work at the phone office to pay for the typewriter. Believe me. I took very good care of it and treated it gently and with great respect.

CHAPTER 4

"What is" is what is.

I had many boys who were my friends. There was Bud, Johnny, Dean and Jackie, but I didn't have any boyfriends. The only time I had been kissed was at a party where everyone was playing "spin the bottle." Like most girls, I dreamed of a prince who would carry me to his castle and we would live "happily ever after." I knew I was not Cinderella, but maybe somewhere there would be a glass slipper that would fit my tiny foot.

In high school I had one date, sort of. Joe was overweight, effeminate and not very well liked. I knew he had asked 17 other girls to the Junior/Senior prom. They had all refused him. I was the eighteenth. Regardless of his faults, at least he was persistent in the face of repeated rejection.

"Donna, would you go to the prom with me?"

"Of course I will," I replied. "Thank you for asking me." I felt sorry for him, but a date with Joe was better than no date at all.

Mother made me a floor length evening gown. Joe brought me a corsage. Daddy loaned us the family car. We gallantly arrived at the high school gym where the dance was taking place. Of course, I couldn't dance. My head barely reached his waist. The miserable evening ended early with a quick kiss planted on my cheek.

When my girl friends, Lucille, Carol and Merry, talked about their favorite subject – boys – I knew I was missing an exciting and special part of growing up, but there seemed to be nothing I could do about it. I tried to be a good sport and pretend that it didn't matter, but deep inside, it did matter. In order to survive this painful time, I turned my attention to other activities. I joined Campfire Girls. I read hundreds of books such as *Little Women* and *Gone with the Wind*. Family entertainment centered on playing cards and games, such as cribbage, pitch and Monopoly. I participated in these games with great enthusiasm. To this very day, I'm still an ardent bridge player, along with computer games and Wii.

I diligently studied chemistry, physics, aeronautics and zoology. While my friends were going to movies and parties with their dates, I learned to enjoy being alone, which proved to be a valuable asset throughout my life.

The effort and energy applied to my studies had their own reward. Although there were only 18 students in my class, I graduated valedictorian. Since the caps and gowns for graduation were rented, Mother couldn't cut one off at the bottom to fit me, so she hemmed it up. The hem measured a foot and a half, but it worked. In fact, I looked quite stunning in my cap and gown as I delivered the valedictory address to a proud audience of family and friends.

It seemed that I was drawn to anything that moved. First it was roller skates, then a tricycle and bicycle. Cars and airplanes came later. Mother called me "Donna Go." As a graduation present, Mother and Daddy had given me, not without some anxiety, a seven week bus trip to California to visit relatives. If they had fears and worries about my safety, I did not notice. I boarded the bus in South Haven on that June day in 1950 just as dawn was breaking, carrying only two small suitcases. My clothes were small, so it didn't take much luggage for them.

I loved to travel and if possible, managed to get a seat in the front of the bus. I spent the first night with friends in Lamar, Colorado, then on to Denver,

Ogden, Salt Lake City, San Francisco, then on to Los Angeles. Everyone was friendly and interesting; the countryside beautiful and enchanting.

My aunt and uncle, Glenn and Reba, met me at the bus station in Los Angeles. The next six weeks were filled with adventure. Glenn and Reba were masters at showing their guests a good time. We sailed to Catalina, bet money at the racetrack, and applauded Mary Martin in *South Pacific*. Another aunt and uncle, Ermal and Lloyd, lived in Ojai. Lloyd and I spent hours playing pitch. We journeyed to Sequoia National Park and sunned on the beach at Santa Barbara. All too soon, it was time to go home.

The trip home was not as pleasant. At the bus station in Phoenix, I ate a hamburger that was less than desirable. In fact, it must have been tainted. A couple hours out of Phoenix, I asked the bus driver to stop the bus and let me out. I had to throw up. He did and I did. This happened several times. I'm sure he was delighted to have me as a passenger. Several of the passengers passed towels to me, knowing the towels would be destroyed from the mess I was in. In the middle of the night, I asked the driver if he could stop for a rest room. Now I had diarrhea, also. The driver knew I was in distress and did whatever I asked him. Somewhere between Albuquerque and Amarillo I found a pay phone at one of our unscheduled stops and called Mother. She said she would meet me at the bus station in Oklahoma City.

Mother had no idea the extent of my sickness, so she made a bed for me in the back seat of the car for the two hour drive back to South Haven. At daybreak the bus pulled into Oklahoma City. Mother was relieved to find me feeling much better. It had been a long night for both of us. It was a long, long time before I would ride a bus or eat a hamburger.

The rest of the summer was spent getting ready to go to the University of Kansas.

The classic question adults ask children is: "What do you want to be when you grow up?"

My answer was always the same. "I want to be a medical technician."

My cousin Sarah had planted this suggestion in me several years before and I kind of liked the ring of it. No one knew much about that profession and tended to discount it. I knew nothing about it, but it seemed easier to stick to that declaration rather than find something else that appealed to me. Mother suggested that I take an accounting or clerical course at the junior college in Arkansas City, 20 miles east of South Haven. Others assumed that I'd continue studying music or piano. The telephone company had offered me a full-time position as a telephone operator. All of the above sounded dull and boring. Besides, my brother Jack had gone to the University of Kansas. Jack was my hero. My stubborn mind was made up. The application to KU was soon in the mail.

Mother bought towels, washcloths, socks and underwear and then dutifully stitched labels with my name on the edge of each. We did the best we could with shoes. They had to be laced up the front for maximum support and sturdy enough to withstand the twisting of my right foot when I walked. There would be a lot of walking to do on the sprawling Lawrence campus. Slacks were easy to make and were matched with shirts and sweaters. Everything I would need was packed into two Samsonite suitcases.

Daddy had me sign a signature card at the bank. I could write checks anytime on his account. Both Mother and Daddy had carefully prepared me, to the best of their ability, to face each of life's challenges fearlessly. There was no resistance or apprehension to leaving home. Going off to college was just the next natural step.

Mother and Daddy weren't quite so confident, but they didn't let me know about their anxiety. Too them, this was a huge step. They knew I would be physically, emotionally and mentally challenged. However, it was just like learning to ride the bicycle. I'd have to discover for myself what I could or could not do. This fear of theirs was never suggested to me. They had to let me go my way, free of any of their preconceived opinions that might influence me. *What a gift they gave me!*

CHAPTER 5

We are responsible for where we put our attention.

Mother, Daddy and I packed the car on September 10, 1950, and headed for Lawrence, Kansas, 250 miles from South Haven.

Daddy carried my precious typewriter and two suitcases to my tiny room. We lingered on the large veranda awhile and finally said our good-byes. I stood on the steps of Templin Hall following their car drive down the winding driveway to Fourteenth Street. A wave of homesickness flooded over me. My eyes filled with tears as I followed the car until it was out of sight. My hand trembled as I reached up for the doorknob and opened the door. Holding on to the door, I pulled myself up the one step into the dorm and began a new life as a college freshman.

It would only be speculation to imagine what Mother and Daddy talked about on their way back to South Haven. Surely they had anxieties about the difficulties I would face. But they never let me know what they were anxious or worried about. They had resolved to set me free years ago. This was just another challenge for them, as it was for me.

The University campus stretched for a mile atop a large hill. In fact, the campus was called "The Hill." The view in every direction was breathtaking. Templin Hall, my dorm, sat a block off campus. In the early 1900s it was a very large, fancy, three-story Victorian home. Later it was remodeled to accommodate 35 young college women. The dining room, kitchen, parlor, library and housemother's quarters were on the main floor. An elegant staircase wound its way to the second floor with 12 rooms and only one bathroom. Each room had a desk and a chair for each student.

Two to four girls shared each room. The back stairway led to the sleeping porch on the third floor with bunk beds and no heat. Many times the windows were open in the winter and snow would dust the sleeping faces. No one complained because we each could have as many army blankets as we wanted. I used seven blankets, six of which were doubled. The seventh blanket wrapped around all of the six. I slid in and out at the top of my bed so I wouldn't disturb the cozy cocoon that encased me. The top bunks were warmer, because what little body heat that circulated rose to the top. The showers were located in the basement. It was impossible to be self-conscious about one's body or body functions for very long. Privacy was not an option.

This would be my home for the next four years.

College was not easy. The adjustment from a small school of 300 students to a college class of over 3000 nearly pulled me under. Even though I was an above average student, so were the other 2999 students. The competition was incredible. A Bachelor of Arts Degree in Bacteriology was necessary for entering the School of Medical Technology at the KU Medical Center after I graduated. So the first semester I took biology, French, English and algebra.

Not only was I mentally challenged, I was physically tested. Each class was held in a different building. The ten minutes allowed between classes were sometimes not enough to get to the next class on time. My English class was on the second floor of Frazier Hall, while the biology class was two blocks away in the Science Building, Snow Hall. With books to carry and hundreds of steps to climb, my stamina was tested daily. My feet ached at the end of the day. Fatigue lulled my tired body to sleep in the warm autumn classrooms. In the dorm, radios, typewriters, laughter and phones ringing destroyed my concentration.

At mid-term, my grade in French was a D. I was stunned. "What's wrong with me? This may be something impossible for me to do. Maybe I don't have what it takes to learn college material." It just seemed too hard for me to ever make it. Heartsick and exhausted, I felt my college days were over. I wanted to call it quits. I wanted to call Mother and Daddy and ask them to come and take me home.

Fear of failure pushed me to re-double my efforts. Maybe I just hadn't tried hard enough. My dear roommate, Judy, volunteered to work with me on those boring French verb conjugations. *Je suis, je ne sais pas.* We made a large chart of all the verbs. She drilled me hour after hour until I had them memorized. I studied like I had never studied before. I ended up with a B in the course.

Since I was ready to quit, I give credit to Judy for pulling me out of my despair. Her willingness to help me may have changed the course of my life.

It was a policy of the University to give parents notice (called a down slip) when their son or daughter received any grade below a C. Mother and Daddy received this notice regarding my French grade. They never mentioned it to me. They knew I was doing the best I could. If I could have done better I would have. Their mention of it would only add pressure on me. That would not have been helpful. One more time, they cut me loose to find my own way.

Saturday nights in the dorm were usually quiet. Most of the girls had dates or were invited to parties. Alone in the dorm one Saturday night, I answered the phone. Several boys were looking for dates. I told the caller that no one was available. "Well, how about you?" he asked.

"I'm not interested," I replied, although a part of me was willing to give it a try. We argued for several minutes. He would not accept "No" for an answer and said he would be over in 15 minutes to pick me up. I dressed quickly and answered the door when he arrived. "I'll go get my jacket and be right back." I told him. When I returned with my jacket, he was gone. I felt a confusing mixture of relief and pain.

Dateless Saturday nights were nothing new. I told myself it was the best night to study because the dorm was quiet. But deep down, I wanted a date as much as any girl. However, another type of call helped me with many of those gloomy, lonely Saturday nights.

A professor called wanting a babysitter as soon as possible. Either they had something come up suddenly or their regular sitter couldn't make it. He sounded desperate. Since I was the only one in the dorm, I told him that I would do it. "I'll be over to pick you up in 15 minutes," he replied. I told him I'd wait for him in the lobby. Dr. Nellick was a gentleman and a good sport. If he felt apprehension or concern I couldn't see it in his face. He courteously opened the car door for his three-foot-ten-inch babysitter. His two children, Robbie and Joan, were six and eight years old, so all three of us were about the same size. This fascinated these children. We all had a wonderful time playing games or reading books. The kind professor probably got an ear full from his children concerning their babysitter. Not only did the children like me, he felt that I was responsible and capable. He continued to schedule me to sit with his children. The difficult Saturday nights had taken on a new and refreshing twist.

My sophomore year was a bit easier. The discipline of learning how to study and concentrate had rescued me from the humiliation of defeat. With my head above water, I could even go to the concerts, attend the KU football and basketball games and participate in other campus activities. College life was finally becoming a pleasure instead of a struggle to survive. I enjoyed the college scene more than the boring summers in South Haven, so I enrolled in summer school between my sophomore and junior years. Since I was planning to be a medical technologist, I applied for a job in the University Hospital on campus. They hired me to work part time in the laboratory. Each student had to take a physical exam at the beginning of their KU experience. So the first week on my new job involved testing over 3000 urine specimens. This operation tested my resolve to be a MedTech.

I had no idea of the change that would soon come in my life.

CHAPTER 6

*We are100 percent subject to suggestion
100 percent of the time.*

Ken, the graduate assistant in chemistry asked me one day, "Donna, have you ever thought about wearing artificial legs?"

"Of course," I told him, "but I would have to have my feet amputated to wear them." I told him of the visit Mother and I had with Dr. Bense many years before.

"Check it out," he encouraged. "There may be some new developments you don't know about."

I liked Ken a lot and we had become friends. In fact, I liked him more than a lot. So, just to please him I wrote to Mayo Clinic describing my congenital deformities. Surprisingly, my letter reached someone who could advise me. He suggested I contact the P.W. Hanicke Company in Kansas City, 40 miles east of Lawrence.

Life was running along fairly smoothly. I was content with it just as it was. Ken had to prod me into writing the nearby prosthetics manufacturing company. "Have you written them yet?" he asked.

"No, I'm not interested in being tall. I'm fine just like I am."

"Donna," he urged, "write them. What have you got to lose?"

Finally, I wrote again describing my physical abnormalities. I immediately forgot the matter.

Until … the next Sunday evening someone called me from downstairs. "Donna, you have some visitors waiting to see you."

Hmmm. Who could that be? I bounced down the steps to meet Betty and Erick Hanicke. My letter intrigued Erick, a skilled German artificial limb maker. Before he had even met me, his mind had created a way to construct legs for me.

Erick had learned this craft from his uncle, P.W. Hanicke. Erick and his brother Werner started their business in Kansas City many years ago. Erick was around 50 years old, a slender man, with dark hair and gentle, intelligent eyes. Betty was younger, with a solid look that said she could deal with any challenge. They directed their business and their energy toward helping people with unusual physical problems. My letter captured their attention. So much so, they wanted to drive the 40 miles to Lawrence to meet me.

We visited in the sitting room making small talk for a few minutes before plunging into the purpose for this meeting. Erick, in his thick German accent told me, "I have thought a lot about your situation. Now after seeing you, I think it will work. We won't have to amputate your feet. We can construct legs for you resembling long boots. The boots would fit over your feet and legs. The artificial knee would be positioned just below the tips of your toes. Your legs would operate similar to a bilateral amputee above the knee, that is, someone who had lost both their legs just above the knee joint. The ankles would be flexible. The toes and knees of the artificial legs would bend. I've never seen a condition like yours. I would have to design and make them by trial and error.

"However, if you're willing to work with me, I'm willing to try. I would like for you to come to our shop. We will set you up on some experimental legs, just to see if you would like to be tall."

We visited for a few more minutes before they left to go back to Kansas City. "Please keep in touch with us," he urged, "and let us know when you will be coming over."

The Hanickes' information certainly added a new slant to my whole situation. Did I take the next bus to Kansas City? No. Was I excited about this new development? No.

"Why would I want to go to all the trouble and expense of wearing legs? I'm doing fine without them, especially since I've learned what it takes to get a passing grade. My life is running smoothly. Why would I want to change it?" This conversation kept going around and around in my head.

Ken was relentless. "So, make an appointment with Erick, just for the fun of it."

His persistence made me wonder, "Maybe Ken would like me better if I were tall."

The summer of 1952 was a hot one. The still nights were stifling. Of course in the 1950s, nothing on the Hill was air-conditioned. The little Emerson fan that Mother and Daddy gave me tried courageously to stir the heavy night air with little success. I spent the mornings working in the hospital lab and the afternoons in bacteriology lab located on the fifth floor of Snow Hall. The 25 Bunsen burners raised the temperature to 105 degrees. The weather forecasters predicted no relief from the heat. I was still resistant to the idea of artificial legs, but thought maybe a change in scenery would offer a distraction from the heat. I called and told Betty that I would be at their shop Saturday morning. Betty's directions to their shop were simple – half a block south of the bus terminal on the same side of the street.

I called a taxi to take me to the bus terminal in Lawrence. When the bus came to a stop on the ramp in Kansas City, I hopped off and headed south. Each shop window displayed something interesting. Suddenly, I stopped in my tracks, frozen. There were wooden legs, back braces, pairs of crutches and a hand that looked as if it had been recently severed from someone's body. I felt like someone had slapped me. I felt horrified and disoriented. "What do these dismembered limbs and grotesque, cold objects have to do with me?" I asked myself. "They belong to people who are handicapped or crippled. I am neither."

Shocked, I had to exercise tremendous control to keep from running back to the bus station. I couldn't just leave. I had to tell Erick I've changed my mind. That shouldn't take but a few minutes. Then I can leave this eerie world and return to the hot, steamy Bacteriology lab, which at that moment seemed like a bit of paradise.

Erick's enthusiasm proved overpowering. He ignored my objections and gently lifted me onto an examining table. "Donna," he explained, "we are just experimenting. We will wrap your legs and feet in plaster of paris. When it hardens, we will attach artificial calves and feet to the bottom of the plaster. We want to see if this will work for you."

In a few minutes the plaster hardened. From a closet in the back of the shop Erick found a pair of woman's shapely legs with nice ankles and stylish shoes. He attached them to the bottom of the plaster. Betty had a full, brightly colored red skirt that I pulled over my head and buttoned at the waist. They stood me up, facing a full-length mirror.

I couldn't believe my eyes. The image in the mirror was a stranger. Smiling back from that mirror was a tall, shapely, stunning coed. The difference was phenomenal. It took a few minutes to realize that the tall, beautiful image was really me. Not consciously, but down deep inside, I sensed that this would be the key to romance.

I was 20 years old and I had never had a date. Well, almost never had a date. I guess you could count the one to the prom in high school. Looking at the gorgeous image in front of me, I was certain my social life would pick up.

I had bought the suggestion that my physical appearance kept me from fitting in with my peers. That was not true. I was embarrassed about my height. This perception of myself kept me from fitting in. It was only my mindset, not reality. Consequently when the opportunity to change my physical appearance came along, I was vulnerable and grabbed on to it like a drowning soul.

Erick watched me closely. Finally, he asked me, "Donna, do you want to be tall?"

My voice trembled with emotion. "Yes, Erick, more than anything in the world I want to be tall. No matter what it takes, I want to be tall."

Betty had the camera handy and quickly took pictures of me standing tall.

Constructing artificial legs required the creative imagination of a skilled craftsman. Erick had that gift. He explained the process to me.

"First, we will cut down each side of the casts that are now on your legs. When the two pieces are put together we will have an exact form of your legs.

This form will be filled with plaster. When the plaster is set, we take the mold away again and we have sculptured duplicates of your legs and feet. We then wrap these sculptured limbs with fiberglass cloth and coat them with resin. When dry, we take them out of the mold and cut a two-inch opening down the front of each. We drill holes along the opening on each side for laces. Your leg and foot will slide into this and lace up as if it were a long boot. Next, we will construct a temporary knee joint, which is used to determine the proper point of balance. Together, we will experiment by trial and error to find that critical point. As you practice walking between parallel bars, I will make minute, delicate adjustments. Once the balance point is determined, a simple one-bolt hinge will replace the complicated knee mechanism. The resin is then covered with leather. The lower legs, ankles and feet are attached. And off you go."

He set to work creating legs that were not only functional and comfortable, but beautiful as well.

I had not told Mother and Daddy of my letter to the Mayo Clinic, the following letter to the Hanickes or the visit with Betty and Erick. Now I could hardly wait to tell them of the decision I had made – the decision to be 20 inches taller! Also, I needed $500 for the down payment.

In my letter to them I explained what had happened to me. I enclosed the pictures Betty had taken that Saturday.

When Mother opened the letter, the pictures fell out. One landed face up on her lap. Shocked, she cried out, "What has happened to Donna?" The artificial legs looked so real she thought they were real! Was this a miracle? Quickly she read the letter. Then reread it. Confused, she called outside to Virgil to come in quickly. Something surreal was happening. She couldn't comprehend what it was.

They read the letter together and stared at the pictures. During the next few hours, questions poured into their conversation. Could Donna handle this physical stress? She had adjusted far beyond their expectations. She seemed happy. She was doing well in school. She had many friends. Wouldn't it be better to leave well enough alone? With a sigh of resignation, Mother finally said, "It's not our decision to make. It's Donna's."

Daddy agreed. I had their full support, along with the check.

Many patients traveled hundreds of miles to reap the benefit of Erick's genius. He could not refuse to help those in need. He adjusted his hours for their convenience. Many evenings he worked in the shop until midnight, laboring over each tiny detail until it was perfect. Saturday and Sundays were normal workdays.

Many a Saturday morning I climbed on the bus to Kansas City to walk on the temporary legs for hours at a time. Finally Erick established the point of balance. This point allowed me to stand comfortably and easily without any support – and not fall down. It was like standing on stilts without holding on to anything. This point was transferred to the permanent legs. I was impatient to be tall and would urge him to hurry. He reminded me that walking on two artificial legs would be difficult. To give me every advantage, his work had to be done flawlessly. The only argument concerned the shape of the lower leg.

"Erick, the calves are too heavy. They make me look like a mountain climber or a football player," I complained.

"No," he insisted, "I like strong, sturdy legs," he said in his German accent. "Erick, I want slim, shapely legs. Trim them down!" I insisted. Finally, he had Betty model her legs for us.

"Do you like Betty's legs?" I asked.

With a twinkle in his eye, he said, "Of course."

"Okay, I want legs just like hers." He measured and whittled until he came very close to the shape I wanted.

Only my three roommates and a few close friends knew of the transformation that was taking place. Others, seeing me leave with my suitcase, would ask, "Where are you going?"

"Kansas City," I answered.

"Again this weekend? You must be seeing someone we don't know about," they teased. "Come on, tell us about him." But I was determined to keep silent until the legs were finished.

Adding 20 inches to my height toppled my whole wardrobe. Short skirts and cut-off slacks would be useless. What in the world am I going to wear? On the next trip to Kansas City, Betty and I went shopping at the "Tall Girls" dress shop.

"I want to try on a skirt that is 32-inches long," I told the saleslady, who looked down at me, confused. Checking each skirt with a tape measure, I pulled all the skirts 32-inches long from the rack and carried them into the fitting room. One by one, I tried on each skirt. The bottoms folded in a pile around my feet.

"I'll take these two. They're perfect." I said. The salesperson probably thought I was off in the head, but I volunteered nothing.

Shoes? The small, crooked shoes would be dumped in the trash. My ongoing problems with shoes had come to an end. I was determined to purchase the popular rage in 1952 – black and white saddle oxfords. I could also choose the size I wanted. Erick molded the artificial foot to fit my shoes. I wanted an ordinary, easy to find 7B shoe size.

Just before the Christmas holidays, Erick applied the last coat of paint and tightened the final bolts. I was uncertain about riding the bus with my new legs, so Ken borrowed a car for the trip to Kansas City. It seemed fitting he would be the first to see me tall, since he had been the spark that started this whole crazy adventure.

Ken was uneasy about the events he had evidently set in motion. He could see more clearly than I could the difficult changes in lifestyle I was about to face. On the way to Kansas City, he gently asked, "Donna, are you ready for this change in your life?"

"Ready?" I replied excitedly, "I can hardly wait!" Any fear of maneuvering on these two new beautiful legs had never entered my mind. My resolve to be tall was unshakable. Ken's resolve was to support me as much as possible.

At 7:30 p.m. December 18, 1952, Ken opened the door of Hanickes at 1009 McGee Street in Kansas City.

I waddled into a dressing room, three-feet-ten-inches tall. I changed into my new tall clothes, a yellow pleated skirt, matching cashmere sweater and black and white saddle oxfords. Dramatically, I threw all of my short clothes in the trash, as if emphasizing the end of an era. I heard Erick come bouncing down the hall with a leg under each arm. I slipped my own legs and feet into each new leg, laced them and then I stood up to my new height. Stunned, Ken couldn't believe his eyes. Betty excitedly took pictures. Erick grinned like a new proud papa. A papa he was to the towering 5'8" girl who had just *grown* 20 inches before their eyes. I felt like I was meeting the world on tiptoe.

Now the hard work began. Every movement I made had to be planned. Every step I took had to be done consciously. Using aluminum band crutches I carefully walked to the car for the hour drive to Lawrence. Ken took the crutches. I lowered myself into the car seat sideways then lifted the legs in. In one hour I would make my debut into the tall world at Templin Hall's Christmas party.

All the lights were on in the dorm when I lifted myself out of the car. Ken handed me the crutches and I inched carefully along the rough sidewalk. It took intense concentration to place the strange new feet in just the right place to move forward. I struggled up the seven steps to the porch. Ken opened the door and I stepped into the room.

Instantly the noisy room became silent. Conversations ceased. "My God!" exclaimed one Catholic girl. Her hands instinctively reached for her rosary. My new legs looked so real that she, and others, assumed that a miracle had taken place.

I had not practiced enough to sit down without tipping the chair over, so there I was, standing tall. I was now eye to eye with everyone in the room. I could smile into each surprised face without having to tilt my head back or yell over the noise to carry on a conversation. I loved this aspect of being tall. I was now on a level with people's faces, not their bottoms! My heart nearly burst with joy and thanksgiving. Even though there was only 20 inches difference, the altitude was euphoric and an entirely new perspective. Everything and everyone looked different. I felt like I had stepped onto another planet, strange and exciting, one of which I knew nothing. I hungered to learn and adapt to this new world. To feel a part of, not apart from, everything that was going on.

Everyone was fascinated to hear the details of what had happened to me. I started at the beginning with my letter to the Mayo clinic nine months earlier, ending with this very exciting night. The story riveted everyone's attention.

"I need to go to the bathroom and I don't know how to get down on the commode," I laughed. "For years I've been lifting myself *up* on the commode. Now, suddenly, I need to let myself *down* on the commode. Looks like I've got a lot to learn about this new tall world. I'll start by climbing those 20 steps up to the bathroom."

Slowly and carefully, lifting each ten-pound, shapely leg I moved toward the top of the stairs, just in time to make the bathroom the focus of my next learning situation.

Aileen, Rosanne and Greta, my roommates, and I talked long into the night. "Can I do this?" I asked, inviting some reassurance.

"Of course you can," Greta encouraged.

"We'll do everything we can to help you," Rosanne added.

And help me they did. Ailie carried my books to classes. Rosanne held the chairs while I practiced sitting down in them. Greta helped me organize my new wardrobe. They all picked me up when I fell, physically and emotionally.

The Christmas holiday break began the next day. Not yet ready to tackle the train for the long trip home, I asked a friend from Wellington, who had a car, if there would be room for me to ride along. There was. I called home and told Mother to meet me at a long-time friend's house. Mother and Daddy saw their new tall daughter when I climbed out of the car and stood up. They were speechless. The silence was palpable.

Finally, Mother's voice trembling with emotion, asked, "How's it going?"

"Fine," I laughed. "But this tall girl sure needs some new clothes!"

Home for the holidays gave me some time to practice some basic living skills, such as opening a door and walking through it or stepping off a curb or going to the bathroom. I learned to open a door by pushing or pulling, then quickly placing my crutch to hold it while stepping through. To step off a curb, I put my crutch down first, then I turned sideways to place my foot by the crutch, moving the second crutch down, then finally, the second foot. Because going to the bathroom was a real struggle, I avoided drinking liquids, especially coffee. Just to stay balanced while I pulled down my panties was the first major accomplishment. Most commodes have nothing to hold on to, so I had to put both hands on the seat, and swing my body around to sit on it. All of these techniques changed as I became acquainted with what I could do or not do.

Practicing at Erick's shop, the various chairs had sturdy arms for support. Therefore, I could control my descent into the chairs. Confronted now with rocking chairs, stuffed chairs, flimsy chairs, lounge chairs, lawn chairs, padded chairs, straight chairs, crooked chairs and, at times, broken chairs, I sometimes decided it was easier to stand. A least my feet didn't get tired.

My brother Delbert and his wife, also named Donna, invited me to go to the Christmas Eve program at the church. As we walked in the church the pre-program commotion suddenly stopped. Silence settled over the sanctuary. Everyone froze. These people, my friends and neighbors, had watched me grow up, watched me roller-skate, ride a tricycle and then a bicycle. Some had attended my graduation from high school. Many had offered silent prayers on my behalf. They had always loved me. Now I was tall. They couldn't believe their eyes.

A few days later, my Aunt Hazel remarked, "You would have thought Jesus Himself had just walked in!"

With the new skirts Mother had made for me packed in my bag, I returned to the KU campus. The first day back to classes was full of challenges. The chemistry professor, Dr. Burkholtz, didn't recognize me and counted me absent. Friends passed me on the sidewalk and didn't speak, not realizing who I was. When I called out their names, they would gaze in wonder at their friend, now tall.

As the days passed the process of walking and living on 20-inch stilts became easier. Little by little, I could do a whole new bunch of movements. I could climb steps, stand at the kitchen sink to wash dishes, drink water from water fountains, see food in cafeterias and use pay telephones. I could work at the laboratory counters at the hospital or in chemistry lab without having to use a stool to stand on.

The most valuable and thrilling event was the ability to be at eye level with those around me. This was the most outstanding aspect of being tall. It somehow made me feel connected and a part of everything that was going on. Maybe this is just a yearning that all human beings have … this urge to feel a connection with humanity, the Planet, the Universe, a Oneness with all Life. I felt like I fit in. That was my payoff. This difference gave me the energy and determination to march through any difficulty or challenge facing me. And there were many.

Hundreds of steps now faced me daily. It started at breakfast, then 20 steps down to the dining room, then 20 steps up to my room, and then 20 steps down for class and seven more steps from the porch to the sidewalk. Forty steps led from the parking lot to the campus. Bacteriology was on the fifth floor. Chemistry was on the second floor. Steps. Steps. Steps. One day I counted the steps I climbed or descended – over 400! Inclines were tricky. I couldn't walk straight down or my knees would buckle and I would tumble. I had to walk down a steep ramp or incline sideways.

Wind, snow, ice, gravel, mud, uneven sidewalks and a hundred other situations demanded intense concentration. Knowing it was dangerous to walk in the snow and ice, I would call a cab to take me to class. When I fell, which I did many times, it was impossible to get up without someone to help me. My roommates accused me of falling only when there was a good-looking man close by to help me up. But the falls were not planned. They were humbling. This "I'll do it myself gal" was learning to accept help from others, with humor and good grace. My independent attitude was undergoing a major overhaul. Also, I later learned to get up by myself when I fell down.

Arriving at the train station in Lawrence to go home for spring break, I discovered the step was too high to swing my leg onto it.

"Sir, could you give me a hand?" I asked one of the boarding passengers.

'I'd be happy to," he replied, as he lifted me gently into the train.

Kind and helpful people were always nearby, if I would simply ASK. I finally understood that my self-centeredness deprived others of offering a small act of kindness. It also cracked my thick shell of self-sufficiency.

CHAPTER 7

*Life sets up all sorts of situations
for us so we can learn.*

Before the summer term came with its stifling heat, I decided to go to the University of Wisconsin in Madison for summer school where my brother Jack attended graduate school. The temperatures and beautiful lakes combined with picking up a few college hours sounded like a great place for a summer vacation.

While riding in the airport limousine from the airport into Madison and the University of Wisconsin campus, I noticed an Arthur Murray's Dance Studio. Dance? Why not?

After settling in at Elizabeth Waters dormitory, I called the studio and made an appointment to talk to them. At the interview, I told them I walked with artificial legs.

"How much do the lessons cost?" I asked.

They ignored me and continued to explain the different steps they taught.

"But, how much are the lessons?" I insisted.

"Miss Hollingsworth," the manager finally answered, "you want to learn to dance? We want to teach you. We won't charge for your lessons."

Of course, they were interested in teaching someone with two artificial legs to dance. I would serve as an example and inspiration to others who believed they couldn't dance.

"Look at Donna," they could say, "If she can dance with two artificial legs, surely you can dance with two good legs."

It was a promotional opportunity they couldn't ignore.

"They want to teach me to dance?" Dancing was one of the most wonderful things that I could not do when I was short. I loved the music. I loved the steps. But I was not tall enough. WOW! I couldn't believe it!

They scheduled me to take a one-hour lesson every day, six days a week for eight weeks. I had to arrange my psychology and art appreciation classes around the dance lessons. My dancing instructor was soon moving me through the waltz, tango, swing step, rumba and samba. I became lighter on my feet as I learned to move my legs to the rhythm with balance and poise.

The University of Wisconsin had a reputation as a fun place to go for the summer. Classes seemed incidental. So, one evening after making an appearance in class, taking a dancing lesson, and sunbathing on the dormitory's top deck, some friends and I decided to walk to town, go out to eat and take in a movie. Any mention of homework was forbidden. We were walking toward the theater when I head a loud pop and fell to the ground. My friends quickly surrounded me.

"Are you hurt?" one of my friends asked anxiously.

"No," I said laughing. But I think I've just broken my ankle.

They helped me to my feet, but I couldn't stand. Yes, the artificial ankle had broken. After my friends helped me to a payphone, I flipped through the yellow pages to find a brace and limb shop. I dialed the number, and even though it was after hours, someone named Bill answered.

After explaining the situation, Bill offered to come and get me and take me to the shop so he could repair my ankle. Since I was helpless, I accepted. He drove me to his shop and inspected the ankle. A cable that attached the ankle to the calf had broken, leaving the foot dangling. He was skilled at his trade and knew exactly how to fix the cable, after which he drove me back to my dorm.

While driving along, Bill asked me a question, "Will you have dinner with me tomorrow night?"

I was nearly speechless. My heart was beating so fast I could hardly breathe.

This was the first time I had ever heard those words. A real date with this attractive young man? I finally answered, "I'd love to."

Bill was in his late twenties and wore one artificial leg. He was personable, intelligent and considerate. He had never met anyone as remarkable as me, or so he said. He wanted his future to include me. We enjoyed going to movies and eating out. At the end of the summer he asked, "Donna, will you marry me?"

What a dilemma! My social life was just beginning. I wasn't ready to marry yet. But what if no one else would ever ask me? "Let's give this some time," I finally told him. We parted at the end of the summer promising to write.

I returned to the University of Kansas to start my senior year. Letters from Bill came often. One evening in October I received a call from him. He said, "If you're free next weekend, I want to come to see you." I didn't have the guts to tell him he was wasting his time. I knew I didn't love Bill. I just loved having a boyfriend.

Bill drove 750 miles to spend a couple of days in Lawrence. All I knew to do was to keep him at arm's length and be cool. I was so cool I never heard from him again. A part of me was relieved. The other part wondered if I should have been more interested in him. What if I had missed my one and only chance?

Well, it was too late to worry about that! But Bill had given me a gift – the assurance that I was desirable and attractive. The phone didn't ring for me, but that didn't hurt anymore.

Since I had gone to summer school, I could take fewer hours during the fall and spring semesters. However, chemistry, immunology and hematology involved many time-consuming laboratory hours. In addition I was still working in the hospital lab. Most of the time I was so tired that every time I sat down, I fell asleep. Professors don't appreciate students sleeping in class and world-renowned hematologist Dr. Cora Downs was no exception. I couldn't stay awake through her boring 8 a.m. lecture.

After one sleepy morning, she said, "Donna, I see you have a problem staying awake. After careful consideration, I believe you are neither physically nor mentally capable of being a technician."

I was shocked and stunned. Hurt and anger boiled inside me. I had adamantly clung to the goal of becoming a medical technologist, even after I found out what it was all about. I had never considered doing anything else.

What does she mean I can't do it? She's probably resentful because I sleep in her class. I'll show her I can do it! Anger and determination gave me the impetus to buckle down and focus my efforts. Dr. Downs had cleverly motivated me to do my very best. She had laid it on the line. I could respond to it or I could react childishly and resentfully. The choice was mine. I earned a B in hematology and my name was on the Dean's Honor Roll that semester.

My roommate, Mary Ann, invited me to go home with her to Wakeeney, Kansas, for the Thanksgiving holidays. Part of their family tradition was to attend a local dance during these special days. Remembering the dancing lessons, I agreed to go to the dance with her.

One unsuspecting young lad asked me to dance with him. Total concentration was necessary for me to follow the steps, so I couldn't talk and dance at the same time. He didn't say anything and neither could I. I didn't dare fall down or we'd both be embarrassed. I was scared. He was surprised. We were both relieved when the silent ordeal was over. He carefully led me to a seat. He wasn't interested in a second dance.

CHAPTER 8

*Joy is watching this Great Intelligence
handle every situation.*

Two months before graduation, I received a phone call from Daddy. I knew
something was wrong when I heard his voice.

"Your mother is in the hospital in Wichita. She had surgery this morning.
They removed a lump from her breast. It was malignant."

It took a few minutes for me to digest this information. A whole gamut of
emotions paralyzed me: fear, sadness, despair, uncertainty. I finally recovered
and told Daddy that I would be home as soon as possible. I started immediately
making arrangements to be gone, probably for a week. The teachers had to be
advised of my absence and give me the next assignments. The next morning
I took a cab to the train station.

Daddy met me in Arkansas City. He filled in the details. "Last Friday
your mother was drying after a bath and felt this lump under her breast. That
same day she went to Dr. Ubelaker. He immediately sent her to a specialist
in Wichita. Surgery was scheduled for Monday morning. Since the lymph
nodes were involved, they did a radical mastectomy. She's doing fine, but
she'll be in the hospital for a few days."

It's not likely cancer suddenly descended on Mother. She had lived for
years with stress and anxiety. Of the four factors involved in health – activity,

nutrition, environment and inner feeling – feelings were the most powerful. She and Daddy lived in a generation where feelings were seldom expressed. Anxiety attacks, crying fits or angry snits were not acceptable or tolerated. Therefore, anger, guilt or fear were not acknowledged or dealt with. These negative emotions had taken their toll on her body. Of course, Mother was not aware of this. She had done the very best she could with the light she had to see by. In fact, she had done an outstanding job of handling life's challenges. She now had another giant issue to deal with.

Daddy had to work at the station. So I climbed on the bus to Wichita and hiked the eight blocks to St. Francis Hospital.

As I walked into Mother's hospital room our eyes met. She knew the tremendous effort required for me to make the trip to her bedside. Neither of us said a word. Our communication was deeper than words. Standing tall beside her there was an exchange of energy, love and understanding. The courage and support Mother had given me for years now silently returned to her.

When I returned home, I took off my legs and stepped into the backyard. My favorite tree and the limb on which I used to sit had grown taller – and so had I. I climbed up, anyway, and sat for a long time in silence. An over-whelming love seemed to fill my thoughts. "The higher you climb, the further you can see. So climb higher, little one, and you will understand more. What 'seems to be' is only an illusion. You are learning to see beyond appearances. This is your lesson."

Although Mother's surgery was extensive and she was taking radiation treatments, she and Daddy made plans to attend my graduation ceremony from the University of Kansas. It would take more than a bout of cancer to keep them away from it!

The university campus sits majestically on a hill overlooking the stadium below. The graduating seniors marched, two abreast, down the winding sidewalk to the stadium where the ceremonies were held. That year there were 3000 in the line. I did not know how fast the others would walk, so I remained near the end of the line in case I couldn't keep up. That was a mistake. The stadium seats filled up, row by row, with the bottom row filling up first, which put me at the very top row of seats. It was a hot June day and my new graduation dress was soaked by the time I was seated. According to tradition, graduates had to walk across the platform to receive their diploma from the Governor of Kansas. Well before my name was called, I began my descent. So, down the bleacher steps I went, then up the steps to the platform. As I approached center stage, the Governor presented me with my diploma. He leaned over and whispered in my ear, "Bless you, my dear."

I certainly needed a blessing. All I could think about was all those steps back to my seat and getting out of that hot robe. Friends told me later that the crowd of 10,000 stood and applauded when I walked across the platform. I hadn't heard it. I probably had too much sweat in my ears.

If it hadn't been for Mother and Daddy, I would have skipped the whole ceremony. But in a way, it was not my celebration, but theirs. The ritual represented a part of the reward for their years of effort and commitment. The journey from seeming hopelessness to freedom and self-sufficiency had been achieved. It was not without trial and pain. My graduation from college was a victory for all of us.

CHAPTER 9

We CAN live fearlessly.

In 1954 a BA degree was necessary to be eligible for enrollment in the School of Medical Technology at the University of Kansas Medical Center in Kansas City. With my hard-earned sheepskin in my hand, I applied, and was accepted for the one-year internship program. Since applications were sent by mail they had no idea that I wore two artificial legs. I wasn't about to volunteer this information. I was required to carry a tray of test tubes, syringes and needles. Some of the procedures would be done at the patient's bedside. Could I do it? Time would tell. The school might not have given me a chance to find out if they had known I was walking on 20-inch wooden stilts.

Judy Koontz and I had developed a warm and congenial friendship during our junior and senior years. Judy was also a bacteriology major, with Medical Technology as her goal. We studied together and bowled once or twice a week at the Campus Lanes. After our acceptance to KUMC, we decided to share an apartment near the medical center.

We found a newly furnished, redecorated, three-room basement apartment, about a mile from the medical center. It was a bit pricey at $75 a month, but we each felt we could handle $37.50.

There were four steps going down to the basement, with a small room off to the side with a washing machine and a clothesline. The living room had new red tile flooring, high casement windows and creamy walls. A small, well-equipped kitchen separated the living room from the bedroom and bathroom. Judy and I felt like we were living in paradise.

The KUMC gave each student $60 a month as lab interns. We felt this was quite generous, since we were actually in school, not employees. Neither of us wanted to ask our parents for money, so we did our very best to make ends meet on our meager funds. Bus fare was 20 cents each way, so we walked to the hospital. We discovered that pork liver at 15 cents a pound was cheaper than beef liver and tasted almost the same. Instead of buying our lunch in the cafeteria at the hospital, we carried peanut butter and jelly sandwiches. This was our first step from financial dependence to financial independence. We each wanted to see if we could make it on our own. We came close. There were two items with which we needed some help: tickets to the Kansas City Philharmonic Orchestra and season tickets to Starlight, an outdoor summer theater production. Living on the edge of poverty, we felt we deserved a little fun now and then.

An internship was easier than college because there was very little homework. All of the training was with real patients, real urine and stool specimen, real blood samples, and real blood donors. The year's program was divided into several services. In the blood bank, we learned to screen donors, insert huge needles in veins and process and type blood samples. The chemistry lab tested for chloride, potassium, calcium, sugar and other chemicals in the blood. Tests for bacteria and other invasive organisms were taught in the bacteriology lab. In hematology, we went to the patients' rooms in all parts of the large medical center to obtain blood samples for specific tests.

Parasitology was the least glamorous of all our classes. We spent eight hours a day crouched over a microscope looking for parasites in smelly feces samples. A month in that odoriferous lab would challenge any student's desire to become a registered technician.

Meeting patients made the month in hematology more interesting. A tray containing syringes, needles, test tubes, glass slides and alcohol sponges was carried to each patient to collect blood samples. I felt very professional in my white, starched, tailored uniform and white shoes size 7B. With my right arm, I carried the tray. With my left arm, I used one aluminum crutch. This arrangement worked very well, at least most of time. Until one day, I had just collected ten blood samples. One more to go on the pediatrics floor and I'd be done. The tray was tucked securely in the bend of my right arm. The left arm was swinging the crutch in perfect timing, when a thought went through my mind, "Don't stumble now, you're almost finished."

At that moment, I glanced down, but I didn't see the wheel of a stretcher turned at 90 degrees parked in the hallway. I tripped and sprawled belly down on the tile floor. Blood and broken glass splattered all over everything within a radius of 30 feet. The noise of the crash brought all the nurses on the floor running to me. They suspected I was mortally wounded as I lay belly down surrounded by blood and glass.

They knelt beside me and asked anxiously, "Are you hurt?"

"No," I answered, mortified at the destruction around me. "I'm sure that's hard to believe. The only thing damaged is my pride and ego for making such a mess."

At least 50 pairs of big, round eyes watched, fascinated, as I managed to get to my feet. I gladly accepted help in cleaning up the incredible mess and began once more to re-collect all the samples of blood.

Collecting blood was usually done in the morning. Visitors were allowed only in the afternoon and evening 2:00 to 4:00 and 7:00 to 8:30 p.m. Facing a long lonely and many times, miserable and scary day ahead of them, most patients were eager to talk to anyone. I had a genuine interest in each of them, and enjoyed these visits. Mr. Evans in room 503 had leukemia. During our daily chats, I found out that he owned the Chevrolet Agency in Kansas City.

"Buying a car is the very first thing I'm going to do when I get a job," I informed him. "In three or four months I'll have a job and I'll check with you at that time."

"May I send one of my salesmen to talk to you?" he asked.

"Not yet. I don't have an income now."

He ignored my comment. "Will you talk to one of my salesmen?" he repeated.

"Okay," I conceded, "I'll talk to him. Make sure he knows he may be wasting his time, because I'm not in a position to buy a car right now."

Several evenings later, a salesman came to my apartment carrying a briefcase loaded with pictures of beautiful cars. Leafing through the pictures I spotted a 1955 red and white Del Rey Club coupe. I almost had a panic attack! "That's it! That's the one I want," I shouted, hugging the picture. "But I don't have any money. I don't have a credit rating. I don't even have a job!"

The salesman seemed unconcerned about the money. He ordered the car, equipped with hand controls for $2,200 I assured him that when I got a job, I would make $200-a-month car payments. He seemed satisfied with this arrangement. He advised me that I would need $180 for taxes and insurance when I came to pick it up.

"One hundred and eighty dollars? That's quite a lot of money on $60 a month," I thought. Then I remembered I had eight $25 war bonds in the family's safe deposit box. That would do it! I called Mother and Daddy and asked if they would get the bonds out of the box and send them to me. They didn't ask what I needed them for. I didn't explain.

Of course, the salesman was not concerned about my ability to pay for the car. The owner of the automobile agency, my friend dying of leukemia, covered for me until I could make the payments. I did not realize this until later, too late to thank him, not only for the car, but also for his trust in me. He would make my payments until I had an income. There are no words to describe the gratitude I felt for these incredible gifts.

The next three weeks crept by. Finally the call came from the agency. The car was ready. My landlord drove me to the Chevrolet dealership. The salesman showed me how to use the hand controls with the left hand. The single lever was attached to the steering column and worked at a 90-degree angle: push forward for braking, pull down for acceleration. That seemed simple enough. I checked my pulse. One-hundred and twenty! WOW! Owning a car was a giant step toward freedom. No longer would I have to struggle onto a bus or train.

No longer would I have to wait for a cab. I could drive, actually drive, anywhere I wanted to! It was unbelievable to me. I felt like I might explode with joy.

Now, over 50 years later, I still have the same euphoria and gratitude for this gift of freedom. Everytime I open my car door and climb in, I sit there for a moment and give thanks to Life for this unspeakable gift.

However, I had one tiny problem. I had never driven a car and I didn't have a driver's license.

I sat down on the seat sideways and lifted my legs in and positioned them under the steering wheel. I started the car and slowly and very carefully eased my shiny new Chevrolet out of the parking lot. Very, very cautiously I inched my way through the Kansas City traffic to the courthouse.

Stepping up to the counter, I said, "I would like a driver's license, please."

"Do you want a regular license or a permit to learn to drive?" the clerk asked.

"I want a regular license." I answered. I filled out the forms and signed them. And there it was – a driver's license.

"The Highway Patrol will contact you in a couple of weeks to come in for a driver's test," the clerk told me and handed me a booklet to study on driving rules and regulations.

I knew I could learn to drive in two weeks. Judy was especially courageous to ride with me to the medical center each morning.

I never heard from the Highway Patrol.

I drove the 300 miles to South Haven the first weekend I had the sporty car. Mother and Daddy did not know I had bought a car. I hadn't told them because I wanted it to be a surprise. I see this differently now. The thoughtful and considerate approach would have been to include them in this momentous decision. They would have been pleased and happy to have been a part of this life-changing decision. I was so absorbed in myself that I was oblivious to their feelings. I regret that. However, maybe Mother did sense what was going on. As I pulled into the driveway, she stepped out on the porch. Her eyes widened with amazement. She was speechless. Two nights before she had dreamed that I had bought a new red car!

October rolled around that year before I was able to start my car payments. It doesn't even need to be said that I never missed a car payment. I would have starved first!

CHAPTER 10

Let Life unfold naturally.

The initial thrill of having a car to drive was gradually replaced by the nagging question of how to pay for it. Here it was the last of May. June 30 would be the last day as a student at the medical center. They guaranteed a job to any graduating technician, but the salary started at $242.50 per month. I had to do better than that!

"How would you like to live in Arkansas?" Judy asked.

"In Arkansas? I've never been there. Why do you ask?"

"I saw this notice on the bulletin board. A hospital in Siloam Springs, Arkansas, is looking for a technician. The starting salary is $400 a month," Judy explained. In 1955, that enormous salary would insure that I would never have any financial worries.

I called the number on the notice and asked if the job was still available. It was. So I left for Arkansas the next morning for an interview.

When I arrived at the Siloam Springs Memorial Hospital the receptionist directed me to the office of the administrator. I looked very professional in my blue silk dress, blue shoes and matching hat. "I want to apply for the job of lab and x-ray technician," I told her. I saw Mrs. Hudson, the administrator, flinch when she saw the aluminum crutches I was using. However, she graciously gave me a tour though the hospital.

When we returned to the office, I filled out the application and handed it back to her. I sensed that Mrs. Hudson was not convinced I could handle the job. I felt her reluctance to offer me any encouragement or hope of being hired. I didn't want to push, so with a cheery, "Thank you for your time," I marched off to see the town.

While sipping lemonade in the drug store, I was surprised to see Mrs. Hudson come in looking for me. She joined me in the booth and explained, "Donna, after you left my office, I felt uncertain and confused. I decided to have Dr. Gunter talk to you." We returned to the hospital where Dr. C.D. Gunter, Chief of Staff, introduced himself. His main interest was orthopedics, therefore, most of the conversation centered on my congenital deformity and the artificial legs. He was fascinated. Finally, he asked, "Walk across the room for me." I did, without crutches. "You do remarkably well on those legs, young lady," he commented.

I really wanted the job. Everyone was kind and friendly. I felt at home in this small Arkansas town. And, I was desperate to find a way to pay for my new car. Maybe the interview with Dr. Gunter would give me a chance.

Mrs. Hudson promised to call after the next day's staff meeting. All of the applications would be reviewed and a decision would be made at that time.

When the call came I was breathless. The receiver was so heavy I could hardly lift it. I was afraid of the hospital's decision, yet, I couldn't wait to hear it. Total conflict. My anxiety level was over the top.

Mrs. Hudson said, "Donna, we want to hire you as part of our staff. How soon can you start to work?"

Relief? Excitement? My mind was spinning. Finally, I collected my thoughts, remembering I had four days of vacation remaining. "I'll be there on June 27.

Later I learned that Dr. Gunter had said to the staff, "I don't know if Donna can handle this job or not, but I feel we have a responsibility to let her try." This was an incredible position for an employer to take. It was as if Dr. Gunter had parted the Red Sea and navigated me across to the land of milk and honey. I couldn't have been more grateful and happy. My heart nearly burst with gratitude.

Judy and Roger helped me pack the car for the move to Arkansas. All of my belongings fit neatly in the trunk and back seat – the faithful typewriter, some books, a few clothes and six new tailor-made uniforms. Although I was leaving friends and familiar, comfortable surroundings, I was fearless. The Ozark Mountains seemed to open their arms and enfold me as I drove the winding roads to Siloam Springs. I felt like the luckiest girl in the whole world.

Mrs. Hudson had found a furnished apartment for me near the hospital. Mother and Daddy drove the 240 miles from South Haven to help me unpack and move into my new apartment. They were interested in seeing the hospital and town. After getting my things in order at my new apartment, we toured the city of 3000 where I would be living.

They were continually amazed at my self-sufficiency, not realizing the remarkable contribution they had made to my independence.

CHAPTER 11

Every challenge is an opportunity to grow.

My title was Supervisor of the Lab and X-ray Departments. The laboratory work was routine – blood counts, blood sugars, chemistries, bacteriology, urinalysis and EKGs. I had one small problem. I didn't know how to take x-rays. I placed the heavy x-ray books in the darkroom and studied whenever I had a free minute. Whenever I had a request to x-ray a patient's chest, I would turn to the index in the book and look under "chest." I would study the pictures to decide how to position the patient. A large chart explained how to set the control knobs on the massive machine.

"Take a deep breath. Hold it." Click. "Now you may breathe."

Legs, chest, arms, fingers, toes, knees, elbows were easy to x-ray, a form of photography. A sub-mandibular joint was a bit tricky. Patiently, Dr. Curl, the radiologist tutored me, but he drove down from Joplin only one day a week. The technician whose job I was taking also helped me. Trial and error proved to be excellent ways to learn.

With my limited knowledge of x-ray, emergencies were terrifying. The first weekend I was on duty was the Fourth of July, 1955. I froze when I heard the ambulances go out, sirens screaming. It could be a long night since I was on-call and sure enough, in a few minutes the phone rang. Even though I was expecting it, I jumped a foot when it rang. I headed to the hospital, heart pounding. When I walked through the emergency door, one victim, apparently dead, lay on a stretcher completely covered with a blanket; another was waiting in the x-ray room. Blood transfusions were needed for still another victim. I took a deep breath. I asked the doctors what they wanted me to do first. Blood was the priority. In a pinch, the doctors could take their own x-rays. So, I started with the transfusions.

The hospital had what they called a "walking blood bank." People in the community interested and able to give blood were typed and the information kept on file. When a patient needed a transfusion, his blood was typed and a donor was called with the same type of blood. To save time, a cross-match could be started while the donor gave the pint of blood, which took about ten minutes. Two a.m. was the ideal time to call donors. They were at home and sensed the urgency of the call. Of course, the donors were proud to give blood and felt like they had saved someone's life, and they probably had. The system worked very well and the recipient was only charged for the lab work and infusion expense. The blood was free – and very fresh! Since blood had a shelf life of three weeks, we couldn't keep a store of blood on hand because it would become outdated before we could use it. The walking blood bank worked very well, although it was a bit stressful for the technician. I really didn't mind since I knew this was very much to the patient's advantage.

Dr. Curl, the radiologist, came every Tuesday to read the previous week's x-rays and do fluoroscopy, upper GI series and barium enemas. Part of my job was to hold the barium can high so the barium would gravity feed into the patient's large intestine. Dr. Curl used the fluoroscope to watch the barium enter the bowel. When we were finished I helped the patient to the bathroom, hopefully before he expelled his bowel-full of barium. We didn't always make it.

One elderly man we worked with was "deaf as a doorknob." Dr. Curl nodded for me to switch off the overhead lights. In the darkness, I screamed in the old man's ear. "We're giving you an enema. Hold it. Don't let it go."

The fluoroscope moved slowly across his abdomen. As my eyes adjusted to the darkness, I could dimly see barium inching all over the x-ray table like a huge amoeba.

"Hold it! Hold your enema," I screamed again in his ear. Still, I could hear the drip, drip, drip of the barium hitting the floor. When Dr. Curl finished the exam and the lights were turned on, the patient, soaked in barium, was clutching the enema tube for dear life. He was simply following instructions "Hold your enema" as he understood them. It wasn't his fault he was in such a mess.

Walking without crutches or canes became my routine. I couldn't climb steps without a handrail or someone to help me, so I carried canes in the car for emergencies. Because I wore the legs so continuously, lumps occasionally developed in my groin area. Sometimes they had to be drained. Beyond that, the legs were comfortable and I was not conscious of them; they seemed to be a part of my body. Many people thought I had had polio because of the way I walked. I didn't bother to correct them. It was just too complicated to explain.

In 1957 I made several trips to Kansas City so Erick could make a second pair of legs. A new outer covering for the lower limbs had been developed that looked like real skin, right down to the toenails. The foot was designed to wear a two-inch heel, which looked very classy. With coordinated skirts and blazers, the result was striking.

The loan on the car had been paid off months before, so I was able to pay for my new legs myself this time. Besides, they were tax deductible.

CHAPTER 12

*There is nothing either good or bad,
but thinking makes it so.*

SHAKESPEARE

Reba, a registered nurse at the hospital, and I became good buddies. Reba had graduated from nursing school in Tulsa. When her marriage dissolved, she and her son Danny moved back to Siloam Springs to live with her parents. We decided to take our two weeks of vacation time in August and drive to Colorado.

We spent the first night with Mother and Daddy in South Haven. The red -and-white Del Rey coupe was ready for the trip, however it didn't have air-conditioning. Knowing western Kansas would be hot, we decided to leave from South Haven at sundown. Although we alternated driving and stopping every two hours for coffee, this was not quite enough to keep us awake.

At 4:00 a.m. on Friday morning, I was driving through Colorado Springs. A sudden jolt and loud crunch woke both of us up. In that split second of sleep, I had run off the road and the rammed into a light pole. The police came shortly, called a wrecker to haul the damaged car to the Chevrolet dealer, and took both of us to the police station. It seemed like the place to go at that time of the morning. I received two tickets: one for careless driving and the other for damaging public property. The court hearing was set for Monday morning at 8:00 a.m.

Since friends in Boulder were expecting us, we climbed on a bus for the hundred-mile trip. Early Monday morning we returned by bus to Colorado Springs for the hearing. Trying to climb on the bus, I stumbled and fell. A young gentleman picked me up and dusted me off. We laughed and introduced ourselves. His name was Jack, "How about a cup of coffee when you get back to Boulder?" "I'd love it," I replied breathlessly.

The courtroom was full that Monday morning. The police had experienced a busy weekend. When my name was finally called, the judge asked me if I were guilty or not guilty to the charge of careless driving.

"Not guilty, your honor," I replied.

"To the charge of destroying public property, how do you plead?" he asked.

"Not guilty." Out of the corner of my eye I saw the policeman who had arrested me signal to me. I had to plead guilty to that charge because the light pole was the tangible evidence of my guilt. Evidently the judge realized that this young lady in front of him was very naïve. He lectured me on driving when sleepy and fined me $100 for the light pole. I was told where to pay the clerk and was then dismissed.

Golden Chevrolet, the dealership, assured me that my car would be repaired in two weeks, in time for the trip back home.

Sure enough, my new friend Jack called the next evening. He was a professor at the University of Colorado with a brilliant mind, beautiful blue eyes, warm smile, ready laughter and a gentle spirit – a very attractive combination. I imagined myself in love, which may have meant that I liked the guy and heard the mating call at the same time. Whatever it was, it was powerful enough to turn my thoughts in the direction of moving to Colorado.

The time had come to ride the bus back to Colorado Springs to pick up the car at Golden Chevrolet. It looked brand new and the insurance company paid for it all. It would not be necessary for Mother and Daddy to ever know the car accident had happened. Besides, who could say that the accident was good or bad or terrible or tragic? Because of it I had met the love of my life. We wrote nearly every day and talked on the phone several times a week. Was this the real deal or was it all illusion? I will never know. I became more convinced that nothing ever happens by accident!

A few months later I applied for a job as a medical technologist at the Rocky Flats Atomic Energy Plant. The interview went well and they agreed to hire me, contingent on my security clearance. Back home, I packed my bags in anticipation of moving to Colorado.

Disappointment came in the form of an apologetic letter saying they doubted my physical ability to deal with the snow and wind in Colorado. I was crushed.

"What do they mean, I can't do it? Of course I can do it."

But their decision was final.

Determined to move to Colorado, I applied for a job at Fitzsimmons Veterans Administration Hospital. This job required a Civil Service rating, which I applied for and was given a GS-7 rating. As soon as a job opened up, I would receive their call.

But Life had other plans for me.

CHAPTER 13

*If we do not respond to the circumstances life
has given us, they will continue to occur.*

Neal Lancaster was a charmer. His troubled past had not destroyed him but had
strengthened and matured him. Neal and his twin brother, Allen, were born April
10, 1911. Allen died when he was nine months old of spinal meningitis. Neal, the
youngest of four other children, was clearly his mother's favorite child. Kathryn,
Neal's sister, told me, "Mother only had one child, Neal." Drinking was not
uncommon, nor was it banned at home. Like an invisible cancer, it insidiously
took control of Neal's life. If he had been asked in high school to set goals for his
life, alcoholism would not have been on the list. It was not his intention to lose
jobs, lose his families, lose his self-respect or try to commit suicide twice. Neither
did he intend to steal from his boss, who was also his brother-in-law, nor end up
in prison after he committed an unspeakable crime of beating up a four-year-old
boy in an alcoholic black-out. These were horrendous events in Neal's life that
destroyed everything in him that was decent. Yet he couldn't stop the momentum
of the self-destruction that not only swallowed him, but caused pain to everyone
around him. His sense of guilt and self-loathing was overwhelming.

The judge in Artesia, New Mexico, sentenced Neal to prison and told him
to never return to Artesia. Artesia residents didn't want his kind of people in
their town.

Six months before his arrest he had cut a clipping out of the *El Paso Times*. It said: "If you want to drink, that's your business. If you want to stop drinking, that's our business." It was signed: "Alcoholics Anonymous." When Neal entered the prison, the authorities found this clipping in his wallet. After a few days, they asked him if he would like to contact AA. At this point, his despair was so great that he was certain he was going mad. He would have agreed to anything. So, in 1947, a call was made to an AA member, who came to the jail to see Neal. He was allowed to leave the prison to go to AA meetings. This was the beginning of a lifetime of service in the Alcoholics Anonymous program.

Eventually, the judge who had run Neal out of Artesia invited him back to start an AA group. His brother-in-law, from whom Neal had stolen, re-hired him to continue in the same job.

In 1950 he returned back to Siloam Springs, married, and on January 28, 1952, his beautiful daughter, Lisa, was born.

The marriage couldn't survive. The divorce was final in 1956.

Neal had found answers to his living problems in the 12-step program of Alcoholics Anonymous. This powerful, highly spiritual program was transformative. To recover from alcoholism, a seemingly destructive, baffling, powerful and fatal illness, would be miraculous. With intense diligence he worked with his sponsor in AA. He was willing to do whatever he had to do to break free from the bonds of alcoholism and insanity. He realized he was powerless over alcohol and that his life was totally unmanageable. Sitting in prison was concrete proof that he was powerless and that his life was unmanageable. He came to believe in a Power that could restore him to sanity. The program suggested a written inventory of his life. Painful? Depressing? Revealing? Of course, but if he wanted to get well, he had to write the story of his life. Self-knowing was necessary for recovery. Part of his recovery involved making amends to everyone he had harmed or hurt. He asked for serenity to accept the things he could not change, courage to change the things he could and wisdom to know the difference.

His dedicated work with the 12-step program healed him. His happy, loving, carefree nature was set free to love his life and the people in it. He found a purpose for living that had a new dimension and a new meaning. He was at peace with himself and the world in which he was living. It was a miracle! He was enjoying living alone and had no intention of getting involved with another woman.

Then he met Donna.

Neal lived across the street from my first apartment in Siloam Springs. He noticed my parents helping me move in on that hot June day in 1955. At the time he thought I'd be an interesting person to know. Over two years would pass before we met.

Mike and Lorraine Moss were my close friends. They encouraged me when the days at work were too long and gave me comfort when I had been at the hospital all night. They made me feel a part of their family. Their neighbor, Odessa Holland, had a room she wanted to rent, four blocks from the hospital. Of course, in a town of 3000, nearly everything is four blocks from the hospital. Mike felt Odessa and I would be perfect for each other and arranged for us to meet.

In her 60s, Odessa had raised five children with wisdom and loving discipline. She was tall and slender, with a wrinkled face reflecting years of hard work and responsibility. Yet her voice, smile and eyes reflected inner joy. Her second husband of ten years had died recently. Her ingrained nurturing nature drew me to her.

We came to an agreement on the room rental of $25 a month, which included all the bills and I could use the kitchen. The arrangement was perfect for both of us.

Odessa knew I wanted to move to Colorado. She listened patiently to all the conversation on how wonderful "he" was and how excited I was to be moving. Odessa helped me when the job at Rocky Flats fell through, softening the blow of that disappointment.

"We don't know the future," she would gently say, "Everything has a way of working out to our advantage. The past is dead. The future is an unwritten page. Let's cherish right now, for that is all we have."

Odessa's words came back to me one October afternoon when my friend Lorraine and I were sitting at their kitchen table and Mike and Neal came in the door. They had been on the golf course all afternoon. This was the first time I had met Neal face-to-face. He was slender, medium height, balding, with happy eyes and a contagious laugh. Everything he said was funny. I found his sense of humor delightful and thought of him as a really fun guy.

When I got back to my room, the phone was ringing. It was Neal.

"I understand you have a girl working for you in the hospital lab by the name of Sally who has a drug problem. Could you meet me for coffee and talk about what we can do for Sally?" he asked.

"Of course," I replied. We made arrangements to meet the following evening at Neal's apartment.

I told Odessa I was having coffee with Neal Lancaster the next evening. Odessa had known Neal and his family for many years.

Her only comment was, "If you don't want to fall in love with him, you better not see him."

I did not cancel the date.

Over a cup of coffee at his kitchen table Neal told me the story of his alcoholism. He left nothing out – the drinking, the three marriages, the many lost jobs, the two attempts at suicide, beating of the boy … jail. He laid it all out, or so I thought, without justification or self-condemnation. That was just the way it was. He did not plan to become an alcoholic. It was something that happened to him and he was powerless to stop it. His guilt and remorse were so painful he drank over and over to deaden the pain. He was trapped in a bottle of self-destruction, with seemingly no way out.

He had just passed a milestone, over four years of sobriety. But still there were no guarantees that he would not drink again. His sobriety was contingent on the maintenance of his spiritual fitness, one day at a time. His participation in the AA program gave him spiritual food, based on the necessity of working with other alcoholics.

Neal had used Sally as an excuse to call me. During our three-hour conversation, he never mentioned Sally. Our first visit ended with an invitation to attend an open AA meeting.

The next evening, Neal picked me up at Odessa's. When I started to open the car door, he gently slapped my hand. "I was taught that a man opens a car door for a woman," he said kindly. This was another opportunity for this "I'll do it myself" gal to learn to accept gifts from others graciously.

The AA meeting was fascinating. The people there, alcoholics and their spouses, were warm and friendly. The talks about their destructive past, what happened to change their lives and what was going on now were open and honest. A lot of their escapades were hilarious in retrospect. To be able to laugh at themselves instead of condemning their behavior was remarkable. As it says in the Big Book of Alcoholics Anonymous, "We are not a glum lot."

After witnessing the many benefits of these meetings, I encouraged Sally to attend. Unfortunately her mind was so befuddled with drugs that she couldn't grasp the program. She disappeared and no one ever knew what happened to her.

Lisa, Neal's six-year-old daughter, was a dear. She was tall for her age, with intelligent eyes, dark hair and the wisdom of 60 years instead of six. She and I liked each other right off. Aware that Lisa might be jealous of anyone capturing her father's attention, I made sure she was included in conversations and activities. By the end of 30 days, seeing each other every night for supper, then on to an AA meeting, Neal wanted me to meet his family.

Kathryn, Neal's sister, invited us to dinner. She and her husband, Bodie, lived in Gravette, 25 miles north of Siloam Springs. I realized I was going for family approval. That thought made me nervous.

After dinner, while helping Kathryn with the dishes, I commented on what a fine person Neal was.

Kathryn abruptly turned to me and said "You don't have to tell me how great he is. I've know him longer than you have."

For moment, I was shaken. Then I realized Kathryn was teasing. Kathryn wouldn't tease anyone she didn't like.

What about the exciting move to Colorado and that heartthrob that had captured my attention? I had almost forgotten about the pressing move to Colorado. The grass was getting greener each day in Arkansas.

During the Christmas holidays, we visited Neal's other sister, Frances, and her husband in Tulsa.

While driving down Riverside Drive on the way to their house, Neal asked, "Donna, will you marry me?"

We had teased and laughed about getting married. In fact, I had longed to hear those words. Now, here they were. The big question. Did I really want to live with Neal day in and day out? Did I really love him? How would he feel about me if I said "No?" It was fun to dream about marriage. However, the reality of marriage was unknown. Minutes passed in silence. I didn't have any answers to the questions I was asking. Then the nesting impulse took over and I said, "Yes."

Both Kathryn and Frances knew of Neal's stormy past. They knew he was in AA and his life was now smoother. They only wanted him to be happy. To them, I seemed wise enough to do my part to make the relationship work and with three marriages behind him, he had, hopefully, accumulated some information and experience that would be helpful. Frances wished us well.

One situation had to be faced before the wedding plans could go any further. Neal had not seen me without my artificial legs. I was used to bouncing back and forth between three feet ten inches and five feet eight inches, but now I was planning to have a roommate that had never seen me short. I worried he wouldn't like me short. What if my body repulsed him? I wondered if he could accept me naked. One afternoon I dressed in my little clothes and invited him over.

I went limp with relief when he held me and said tenderly, "Donna, your legs make no difference to me. It's you that I love."

We talked about having children. As far as I knew, I had all the necessary equipment to conceive and carry a child. Although my periods had not begun until late in my teens, they had been regular. A caesarian section would have been necessary instead of natural childbirth because of the shape of my pelvis and lower back. We decided not to have children because of our age difference and the possibility of problems associated with childbirth. Neal volunteered to have a vasectomy, which made the decision final. Besides, we had Lisa.

Lisa was beginning to suspect that her beloved daddy was planning to marry me. One evening after our favorite meal of hamburgers and french fries, Lisa asked Neal to sit in his big chair, with me on one arm of the chair, while she sat on the other.

She then laid a big Bible on his lap and asked, "Daddy, do you really love Donna?"

"Yes," he replied.

"Would you be happy married to Donna?" she continued.

"Yes." Neal said.

"If you marry Donna, do you promise, on the Bible, you will never fuss with her?"

Lisa then asked me the same three questions, getting the same answers.

Then she proudly announced, her bright eyes shining, "I think it is just great for you two to get married."

I had answered the questions Lisa asked and gave the answers I was expected to give. But this marriage situation was uncharted territory. Did I really love Neal? He was considerate, patient, fun and seemed reasonably responsible. I liked him. But love? I really didn't know what that meant.

I suspected there was more to it than having fun in bed, but the question about happiness? I had no clue what happiness was. Happiness had to be more than having everything going my way or being comfortable all the time. That would certainly not be realistic. Excitement was not the same as happiness. Excitement was too nebulous and short-lived. Happiness, peace, serenity, joy – these words were ill defined, yet seemed worthy of attaining. Happy with Neal? That, too, was an unknown. And the last question about not fussing? Neal seemed easy going, but, 24 hours a day, seven days a week? I couldn't even say that my own emotions would never erupt into anger, resentment, sulkiness or irritability. That would be asking a bit too much. The only thing I could do was to do the best I could do. I felt like I was jumping out of an airplane without a parachute.

Mother and Daddy knew nothing of the whirlwind courtship between Neal and me. In fact, they knew very little about my social life. As far as they knew I had never had a date. Marriage was never considered. So, when I called and said, "Neal and I are getting married. Is it all right for us to visit you this weekend?"

They were stunned. The silence on the other end of the phone was interminable. Finally Mother managed to say, "Of course. We'll be expecting you."

"Donna married?" It took some time for this to resister. "A son-in-law?" This was a whole new area of speculation and suspense. What kind of a person was Neal? Knowing me as they did, they had better like him, because my decisions were usually set in concrete. To raise any objections would be useless.

To their delight and relief, Neal was charming and likable. He had a remarkable ability to put other people at ease, so everyone had a good time. He was even willing to learn to play pitch, a game the family had played for years. Politely, Neal asked Daddy if he could marry their daughter.

Daddy had only one comment: "Be good to Donna." Mother had one question for me, "If something happened to Lisa's mother, would you be willing to raise her as your own?"

"Yes," I replied, "Lisa is everything I would want in a child of my own."

The day before the wedding, Neal and I went to the bank to put our accounts together. When the teller showed us our accounts, I had several hundred dollars. I looked at Neal's account in disbelief. He had $1.37. I was surprised. He was relieved that he was not overdrawn. One thing was certain: I was not marrying him for his money!

The date was set – February 23, 1958, at 4:00 p.m. in the Methodist chapel. Roy, Neal's long-time friend, was best man. Reba, my friend who had vacationed in Colorado with me, was matron of honor. The guest list was simple: Mother, Daddy, Delbert and his wife, Donna, who came from South Haven; Neal's brother, John, and his wife, Polly, from Ponca City; Kathryn and Bodie drove down from Gravette; Frances and Doc arrived from Tulsa; and of course, Odessa. All of Neal's relatives were relieved he had found someone as delightful and responsible as me. My family was somewhat cautious. Very little of Neal's turbulent past had been disclosed to them.

Neal's previous marriages had ended in disaster, yet here he was at the altar again. Doubts had been crowding his mind as to whether he was capable of making a marriage work. He loved me so much that he was terrified he would fail once more. It was too late to back out now. He earnestly prayed he would not hurt me. His hand was shaking when he took my hand to say the marriage vows we had memorized. In a few moments it was all over as the minister said, "I pronounce you husband and wife."

Odessa had prepared a reception at her home for the wedding party. Cake was cut and served along with non-alcoholic punch. Pictures were taken. Everyone put their concerns behind them and celebrated this union. Everyone wished Neal and me a happy life.

CHAPTER 14

We would feel fantastic and enjoy ourselves
if we dropped all expectations.

Neal had been living in a three-room furnished apartment above a garage, which rented for $25 a month. I moved in, made new curtains and painted the cabinets. While I was re-arranging the closets, I noticed all of Neal's ties were tied and the short ends cut off. How strange. When I asked him about this, he explained that he could not tie his tie. So he had someone else tie it for him. He would then loosen it just enough to slip it over his head and pull it around his collar. The longer he followed this routine, the longer the short end became, so he had to keep cutting off the short end to keep it from showing below the long end. Simple solution to a knotty problem! We both laughed hysterically.

Neal helped me with everything except the cooking. If our day at work had been busy and long, we ate out. We both enjoyed having a clean, uncluttered environment. We placed dirty socks in the clothes hamper and shoes neatly in the bottom of the closet. We made the bed before we left for work.

I was on call five nights a week and every other weekend. When the hospital called me in the middle of the night, I moaned, groaned and complained. My exhausted body resisted getting dressed and going to the hospital for God only knew how long. Patiently, Neal would get dressed and go with me.

During a phone call, Neal's brother, John, asked how we were getting along.

Neal said, "We're getting along great! I let Donna have her way in the things that matter. She lets me have my way in the things that don't matter!"

There were some tough lessons to learn, however, such as accepting another person, just as he is. Neal was rarely out of sorts, but when he was, I wanted to fix him, basically because I was more comfortable when he was happy.

"What's wrong?" I asked, assuming it was something I had done.

"Nothing's wrong," he grumbled.

I had to learn to let him be responsible for his own mood, without my interference. Likewise, Neal had to let me work out my own conflicts. It required practice to stand back and let the other person be free. Fortunately, we each had 12-step programs to help us learn these new skills.

In the late 1950s we started a 12-step program for families and friends of alcoholics. We used the same transforming steps the AA groups used. An in-depth study of our inner state revealed areas of conflict which could be resolved with being ready and willing to have these defects removed. The program also advised a continuing inventory and a search for a closer relationship with a higher power.

Being aware of the times when I was controlling and self-absorbed, like a child wanting its own way, helped to smooth out many bumpy spots in my relationship with Neal. To be able to recognize the times when I wanted to tell him what to do, when to do it, how to do it, what to wear, how to act, uncovered my own need to have things my way. I watched myself project guilt when I cleaned out the garage at a time when I knew he would catch me doing it. That would surely make him feel guilty, because I had asked him several times if he would clean it. I observed myself blaming him when things went wrong. One weekend we had traveled to Blytheville, Arkansas, to attend an AA conference. I had packed a travel iron in case of an emergency. Neal asked me to press his jacket, which I did. While the iron was still hot, I decided to press the collar of my dress. When I did, the whole collar burned out. Of course, my first thought was, "If Neal hadn't asked me to press his jacket, I wouldn't have ruined my dress." What nonsense!

I also learned from this 12-step program that if I refuse to make a judgment, I will not be resentful or angry. This sent me searching for the basis of judgment. I found that when I know that another person is doing the very best they can do at a given moment, with the experience, wisdom and information available, I make no judgments. This may not be what the person is potentially capable of, but at that moment, they could not do it differently. The same is true for me. If I can accept the *fact* that at a given moment I am doing the best I can do, I then free myself of guilt and Donna bashing. In these weekly meetings I learned about how dangerous, destructive and self-defeating it is to play the victim role. All of these insights helped me to grow up.

When we had an invitation to go out with friends, I became tense.

Neal's reaction to plans of any kind was resistance. His initial response was, "No."

After a while, I learned to say, "That's okay, you do whatever you want to do. I believe I'll go."

Reluctantly, sometimes he decided to go with me. He usually ended up having more fun than anyone else. Occasionally, he stayed home and I stayed home with him. Gradually, we learned to give each other the freedom to do what we each wanted to do, and not feel guilty. I played bridge every Monday night. Neal never objected. We tried never to place unreasonable demands on each other. Most of the time, we succeeded.

CHAPTER 15

If we are not looking for the ideal,
it is easy to make a decision.

House plans were beginning to cover the kitchen table. This was the first symptom of house heat. The apartment was cheap and comfortable, but the time had come for a real home. We mentioned this desire one evening during dinner with Leon and Cleo, who lived at Lake Frances, six miles south of Siloam Springs. They knew of a real bargain, just down the road from them

"This house and seven lots near the lake can be bought for $1,500. It's a real steal," Leon said. "Let's go look at it."

The single lane, rutty road was a bit of a chore to maneuver, but once we were down the hill to the little cabin nestled in a stand of pine trees, we could see that, with a little stretch of imagination, it had a lot of possibilities.

The leaky roof, knotty pine walls, screened in front porch, falling down back porch and a fireplace that didn't work captured my interest. Neal, more realistic than I, didn't have the same reaction. It looked like an overwhelming remodeling job to him. The plumbing was clearly marginal and septic system barely functional. After assessing the work required, the initial price of $1,500 was the least of the expenses.

Leon knew the owner and arranged a meeting to discuss the sale of this cottage in the pines. While discussing the sale price Neal, with very little enthusiasm, said, "There's no way we'll pay that price. $1,350 is our top dollar."

When the seller looked at me I had big tears in my eyes, he knew the sale was in the bag. Sold – at $1500. The house was on land that could possibly be divided into seven lots with uncertain boundaries. There was also a view of Lake Frances if you had the courage to stand on a ten-foot ladder placed in the back yard.

The work began. The dark wood floors were sanded and refinished. They turned out to be a beautiful white pine. A light colored tan stucco was applied to the outside walls with matching brown trim. The new roofing matched the stucco and trim. We started over in the small kitchen with a built-in oven, food bar, new sink and cabinets and new refrigerator. The back porch was torn off and replaced with a 20 foot by 20 foot sunroom, with nothing but windows on three sides. We poured a 14 foot by 20 foot patio in the back yard and added a carport.

We hired someone to do most of the work. However, I wanted to paint the trim on the screens, all 40 of them. My plan was to spend my two days off working on this project. Once the task had begun and momentum kicked in, I decided to go as far as I could before I had to clean the paint brushes. By the time Neal rumbled down the rocky road at 6:00 p.m. I had just finished painting screen number 40. Barely able to lift my arms and covered in brown paint, I proudly showed Neal the stack of neatly painted screens.

There were several drawbacks to this paradise in the country. In the winter, the road was almost impassable. Also, I was on call at the hospital, which meant a six-mile drive to the hospital that often took over ten minutes. An outside bell was installed to the telephone so I could hear the phone ring when I was in the yard. Since we lived in the country, our telephone was on a line with four other parties, which was not always convenient.

One time I was cooking spaghetti and cheese for dinner when the hospital called. Someone had fallen and they needed an x-ray. The spaghetti was already cooking when I left and I forgot to tell Neal when to take it off the stove. Ten minutes later he tried to call the hospital to ask me what to do, but someone else was using our telephone party line. Finally, in desperation, he interrupted the conversation and asked, "Can one of you ladies tell me how long to cook spaghetti?"

"Cook spaghetti?" someone on the line said.

Neal explained what he needed and they laughingly told him.

We enjoyed eating our evening meals on the patio watching the wrens, cardinals, chipmunks and other fascinating wildlife. Occasionally, we would see a copperhead or a stinging scorpion.

Then there was Molly, our two-year-old female boxer. She could not stay in the house while we were at work, so we built her a doghouse that matched our cottage. She didn't like her new quarters. I even crawled into her house with a tasty morsel of steak and tried to get Molly to crawl in with me. Molly wouldn't budge... until... one very cold morning when the temperature was about zero degrees. As we drove out of the driveway, we saw Molly's eyes, peeking out from behind the carpet we had hung over the door of her cozy nest.

Molly also insisted on sleeping on the couch in the living room, which we did not approve of in our tidy home. We never could catch her on the couch because she waited until we turned the light out and went to bed. So we finally set a mousetrap on the couch.

Just after the light had been turned off, we heard this racket and commotion in the living room. When she leaped onto the couch, the trap sprung. She was so frightened that she got the message. The couch never interested her again.

At 5:15 Molly would start pacing back and forth because she knew Neal would be home within minutes. Neal loved her so much that he spent time playing and running with her. She was an intelligent and delightful companion except when she passed gas, which nearly drove us out of the house!

Neal decided to get involved in politics. He joked that it seemed easier than working for a living. He filed to run for the position of City Clerk and Treasurer, a very courageous undertaking for him. Neal had been born and raised in Siloam Springs. Even though he lived in New Mexico several years, most of the people in this Arkansas town knew he had a problem with alcohol. He was still drinking when he returned to his home town in 1950. His last battle with the bottle occurred in September of 1952. In this small town of 3000, secrets were almost impossible. Alcoholics Anonymous was NOT an anonymous organization. If Neal was seen at the coffee shop with someone, the town seemed to know that AA had a new member in tow.

Neal filed to run for the position of City Clerk and Treasurer. It was common knowledge that he was a sober member of AA. Nevertheless, it was questionable whether he would have enough votes to defeat his opponent. A politician at heart, he overwhelmingly won the election.

However, a city ordinance required he live within the city limits. Reluctantly, we listed our country home and property for sale. Even though it was on a dead-end road that was nearly inaccessible in the wintertime, once found, it was a prize. Potential buyers just could not see it through our eyes. We sold it at a stinging loss.

Fortunately we both had good incomes, which totaled $800 a month. In the early sixties, our banker thought this was more than adequate and loaned us $16,500 for a new home.

We built a three-bedroom brick home in the south part of town. This project took the edge off of our sadness in leaving the country. We adapted quickly to central heat and air conditioning, paved street, wall-to-wall carpeting, city sewer system, garbage disposal, washing machine and clothes dryer. Since I seldom wore my artificial legs at home, we had the carpenter build a pullout shelf in one of the lower kitchen cabinets, which served as a workbench for cooking.

Our home was warm and friendly. We had many friends who, with very little urging, came for the weekend. These guests now had their own bathroom in which the lavatory would drain and the stool would flush.

Life was very good.

Jack, Delbert and me, Kingman, Kansas, 1936

Neal and me, 1959

Daddy, Mother and me, 1954

Donna, age 14

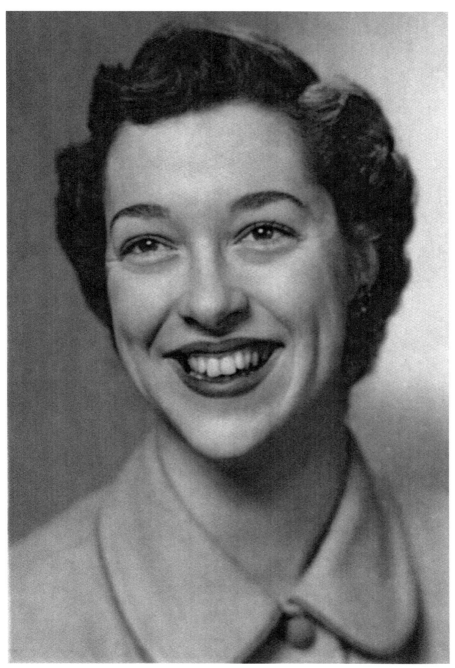

My high school graduation photo, 1950

Donna, 1952

Donna at piano, Templin Hall KU, 1953

Templin Hall, KU, 1953

New car! 1957 Buick Special

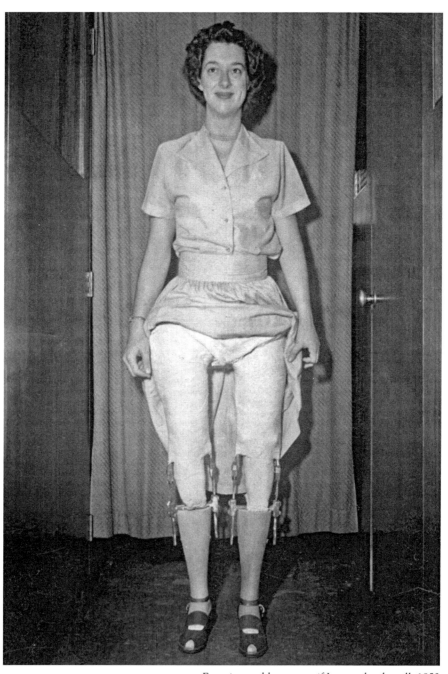

Experimental legs to see if I wanted to be tall, 1952

On my deck in Whitney, Texas, 2002

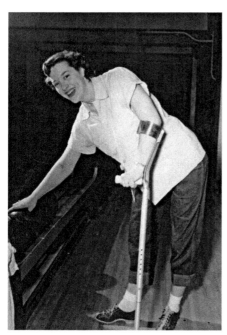

Kansas University. Bowling at Student
Center, 1954

Jet East Dallas. My experimental aircraft –
N74066, 1990

After I took my friend Margaret for a spin, 1994

Donna, 2009

CHAPTER 16

Inner conflict is dangerous and fatal.

Nearly every month we drove to South Haven to see Mother and Daddy. Mother was not well. She had gone to the doctor with pain in her back, shoulders and arms. He was treating her for arthritis. Because the pain continued, the doctor finally sent her to a bone specialist for a check-up and x-rays.

The next Sunday morning, Daddy called and said, "Your mother is in the hospital for treatments. The cancer has spread into the lungs, bones and God only knows where else. The treatments she is taking will not cure her, only help to control the pain."

I felt like a knife had just been plunged into my stomach. I knew my mother was fatally ill.

Neal and I went to church that morning. I quietly wept throughout the service. By the time the service was over, a calm acceptance had replaced most of the horrendous pain. Wanting the situation to be different would not make my mother well. "What is" is what is. Resisting "what is" is insanity and accomplishes nothing, it only makes things worse. I intended to be as cheerful and helpful as possible and perhaps these last few months would be easier for all of us. Each weekend, Neal and I drove to South Haven to spend precious time with Mother and Daddy.

As long as she was able, Mother baked a chocolate pie each Saturday and had it waiting for us. At times, Mother would bake the crust, then rest; make the pudding, then rest; then finish with the meringue. She was totally free of self-pity and never complained. She was consistently cheerful and optimistic. Since she was always ready to play cards or games, we had many wonderful evenings.

Then the time came when she couldn't make it to the bathroom or to the table to eat. Daddy had his hands full with laundry, meals and caring for her. He would never have asked me to come home to help him, but was genuinely pleased when I offered and came to stay with him until it was over, until Mother died.

It was not easy to watch her body slowly waste away from the lack of food, but she couldn't eat. If she could have, she would have. But she could not. Mother knew, as did the whole town, that she was dying. It was not a secret. However, like religion, death and dying were never discussed. Daddy took the position that her dying would not be discussed around her. So the subject was discussed only on the front porch so Mother couldn't hear it. We did, however, take care of her and maintain a pleasant atmosphere. Hundreds of friends came bringing food or flowers, showing their love for her. The physical acts of caring were obvious from everyone. The sharing of this very personal act of dying was missing. Unfortunately, that was just the way it was. The concept of hospice had not surfaced yet.

Years later, when I realized the value of talking to the dying about dying, I worked with hospice as a volunteer, both in Dallas and, later, in Whitney. In some small way, I made up for not being available to Mother before she died. It was one of the most rewarding activities I ever engaged in.

Neal came over from Siloam Springs every weekend. He loved Mother as she did him. I had been her greatest concern for 30 years. She was peaceful with the knowledge that Neal would take care of me.

She died as she had lived, with courage and acceptance. The whole town came to her services to celebrate her remarkable life.

CHAPTER 17

*If our attention is not on this moment,
our awareness is fragmented.*

Eleven years passed since I had started to work at the Siloam Springs Memorial Hospital. Although I had worked my way up and earned a salary that allowed us to have many comforts, I was at the point where I didn't want to go to work. I watched the clock and counted the minutes until quitting time. I felt put upon when a child broke their arm and needed an x-ray just as I was leaving to go home. I pulled the covers over my head and groaned when the phone rang at night announcing a call from the hospital. The most satisfying part of the week was my time off. The enthusiasm and creativity I once had were gone. These were compelling signals that it was time for a change. So, I quit my job.

I didn't quit before I had another one, however. The medical clinic adjacent to the hospital needed a lab and x-ray technician. The salary was better, the hours more regular and the work easier. I applied for the position and got it. There were some drawbacks, though. The winter of 1968 was bitterly cold. The clinic didn't have central heat and air-conditioning; they just used an open space heater. On one particular night the wind had shifted to the north and when I arrived at the office the next morning, it was freezing cold. Shivering, I turned on the heater and stood with my back to it, trying to stay warm. In a few minutes I smelled something strange. I then realized I had been too close to the fire and the calves of my artificial legs were burning. The stockings on them had melted and the paint was blistered. Luckily I only needed sandpaper and paint instead of an emergency room because something was about to happen to Neal and me that would dramatically change our lives. The benefits of this new job, more time, more energy, more money, would help to make our new adventure possible.

It all started when we decided to take a vacation before I started the new job at the Clinic.

We had friends in Big Piney, Wyoming, who had urged us to visit them. So we took them up on the invitation and spent a week in the beautiful Wyoming mountains. On our way home, the highway seemed to stretch endlessly before us. It was going to be a long day of driving. "I wish we could fly," I wearily sighed.

"Why don't we?" Neal replied.

Something happened inside of me. At that moment, an excitement began to build into a realization that flying was not impossible – even for me. I knew there was an unseen force that allowed an aircraft to fly. That's why I took aeronautics in high school so I could understand this incredible phenomenon. It was so simple. Because of the shape of the wing, the wind flows faster over the top than it does under the wing. This creates a vacuum or an area of low pressure that generates lift.

When I was a child, my older brother, Delbert, returned from the service and he started taking flying lessons. I was always ready to go with him to the airport, just to watch the planes take off and land. One day, his instructor offered to take me for a ride. I had never forgotten this magical experience. Now, the remaining miles on that hot July afternoon seemed to just whiz by as I began to accept the possibility that maybe, just maybe, I could learn to fly.

Our close friends Roy and Erma influenced our decision to learn to fly. Roy, Erma and Neal had grown up together in Siloam Springs. When Roy returned from California in the early sixties, he was a shaking, sick and miserable alcoholic. Neal became his AA sponsor. They traveled to AA meetings nearly every night. Roy never drank again. Erma was co-owner with her brother of Allen Canning Company east of Siloam Springs. Roy and Erma fell in love and married. The canning company needed a plane and pilot. Roy had always wanted to fly and filled this position with great passion.

Flying consumed his every thought and word. My attention was riveted to his every word, fascinated with his flying stories.

Erma's legs were paralyzed, the result of a back injury when she was a young girl. Roy had designed some hand controls for the brakes and rudders, and after having them custom made, installed them in their Cessna Skylane so Erma could learn to fly also. Roy knew similar hand controlled brakes and rudders could be made that would work for me. So, the first step, we decided, was to buy an airplane. Roy suggested we call Ed Reeve, a skilled flight instructor at the Siloam Springs Airport (now called Smith Field). Ed knew of a Skyhawk in excellent condition for sale at the airport. He felt it was worth the asking price of $6,000.

The next morning, we went again to our friendly banker and borrowed money to buy a plane, which neither of us could fly. He didn't even ask us if we could fly the plane before he loaned us the money to buy it.

"Ed, now that we have this airplane you recommended to us. I need to learn to fly it. Can you teach me to fly?" I asked him hopefully.

"Can you drive a car?" he asked.

"Of course I can," I answered.

"Then you can learn to fly," he said.

With intense excitement, I told my co-workers at the medical center, "We bought an airplane."

"You what?" they asked in a tone that indicated we were mad.

"You don't know how to fly a plane," they teased.

"Of course we don't. We can't even start it!"

"You guys are crazy," they concluded, shaking their heads.

Flying, as I discovered later, was not quite as simple as driving a car, nor was Ed as confident as he had led me to believe. He was however, wise enough to avoid any suggestions that might dampen my enthusiasm. He sensed the belief in my ability and the intensity of my desire would overcome any and all obstacles. He was right.

Roy worked with us to design the hand controls and an ironworker in town made them. A metal plate was clamped on to each of the foot pedals. From this plate, a rod extended upward. There were short handles on the top of each rod, which rested on the seat between my legs. With my hands, I could use each of the rods, independently or together, pushing forward for brakes or pressing downward for rudder control. But first, I had to learn the function of a rudder!

July 24, 1971, 5:00 a.m. The airport beacon was still making its knife-like sweeps through the countryside as I drove down the narrow lane to the hangar. I was meeting Ed for my first flying lesson. I had to learn how to pre-flight the 1960 Cessna Skyhawk to insure safety of flight. We looked at the air pressure in the tires while walking up to the plane. It would be embarrassing and dangerous to land a plane with a flat tire.

The gas cap was unscrewed and a long stick was dipped inside the tank, then pulled out to confirm the tank was full. The cowling was opened and the oil checked. The engine had to have oil pressure to operate, so the dipstick was securely locked into place. Gasoline can't have even a few drops of water in it, so a sump button drained away any water. The prop was felt for nicks by running my hand along the leading edges. The rudders, ailerons and control wheel were checked for freedom of movement. *And, oh yes, check for bird nests in every small opening.*

Ed guided me though the pre-flight checklist, then watched as I maneuvered the rudders to turn the plane right or left. We taxied to the end of the runway. The plane was equipped with dual controls, so Ed could take over, if necessary. We checked the sky for any other planes in the pattern. The sky was clear. So we gradually pushed in the power. The plane moved slowly at first then gained momentum. In a few moments the tiny craft lifted from the runway and we were airborne. To my amazement, flying was more fun that I ever dreamed it would be. The view was breathtaking. We leveled off at 3000 feet and practiced simple maneuvers, such as going up, down, right or left. Time was up too quickly for this first lesson. Ed smoothly squeaked the plane back onto the runway.

I had no illusions about becoming a famous pilot. I just knew that flying was something special, which justified spending all the money, time and energy I could muster. The stirring within had something to do with an innate sense of freedom.

I was born with a free spirit, which somehow seemed trapped in a body, a job and the conditioning of my upbringing and society around me. Flying seemed to diminish these limitations. It was like dis-identifying from the world and just observing it, rather than being emotionally involved in all its problems. This produced exhilaration beyond measure. This airborne world of order, harmony and peace seemed much more real than the illusionary world of heartache, misery and limitation.

Everything in flying is a learned reflex action with one exception … instinct. Instinct keeps the pilot from flying the plane into the ground. Starting the engine was a pattern that had to be repeated over and over until the sequence was established and automatic. Attention was required to remember that the wingspan would easily bump into buildings or other planes. The tail section stretched behind me and the propeller was a lethal weapon. Throughout the lessons, Ed gave me information he had acquired from his 20,000 hours of flying experience.

"I'm teaching you a sequence of actions which will result in safe flying. Follow it implicitly. Your life may depend on it."

During some lessons, Ed would say, "Isn't it a beautiful day?" This would challenge my concentration to hold the wings level, airspeed constant, altitude steady, heading right on course, talk on the radio – all of these activities had to be controlled at the same time. The lessons stretched my mind and ability. Eventually, after hundreds of flying hours, I could carry on a conversation, manicure my nails and fly the plane all at the same time.

When I started the flying lessons, the other pilots at the airport had been skeptical and aloof. They believed that to fly with hand controlled brakes and rudders would be dangerous and impossible. They thought my flying was just a brief fling. I'd soon realize how difficult it was to maneuver the craft without using my own legs and feet. Although I always flew with my artificial legs on, they were useless to operate the foot pedals. Faced with these difficulties, the guys at the airport expected me to lose interest and quit. With apprehension, they watched as I spent hours and hours practicing this skill, which required hard work and focused attention. In a few weeks they understood, as pilots, my fierce determination to learn to fly. Then they eagerly gave me their support and shared their experiences. These pilot friends had never seen a student with hand-controlled brakes and rudders fly a plane. Realizing it would require a great deal more skill and perseverance to fly a hand-controlled aircraft, they watched me practice landings with great concern for my safety. They really wanted me to make it.

On August 23, 1971, Neal said he was going to the airport with me for my lesson. I was suspicious. I had less than 20 hours, but the time had come for me to solo. This meant flying the plane alone. There would be no one in the right seat to take over if I messed up. As pilot in command of an aircraft, three takeoffs and landings had to be made to qualify to fly the plane solo.

Sure enough, after a couple of swings around the flight pattern in the cool, calm morning air, Ed asked me to stop the plane near the taxiway. He crawled out of the cockpit, looked up at me and said, "It's all yours. Good luck!"

There I was, alone, with the instructions to make three takeoffs and landings. My heart was racing and I could hardly breathe.

Then, very carefully, I taxied to the end of the runway, radioed I was departing Runway 36, released the brakes and pushed in the power. The plane began to move down the runway. When the speed was sufficient to support flight, I gently pulled back on the wheel. The aircraft lifted gracefully from the runway. Within seconds the tiny craft and I were airborne. Would I ever get it back on the ground without crashing it? Probably not. I realized I had to focus my attention on the techniques Ed had taught me. I reduced the power setting to 80 RPM, then entered crosswind and turned on final approach. I cut the power, raised the nose of the plane very gently and carefully. The plane settled over the runway.

I heard the squeak of the tires. "Whew! Two more landings to go." Drenched in sweat, adrenaline pumping and a bit of confidence emerging, the next two were over without killing me and/or wrecking the plane.

I taxied up to the ramp, opened the door of the plane to climb out and was suddenly surrounded by a huge crowd. The other pilots hugged me and cut off my shirttail to hang on the office wall, as is the custom for those who have just soloed. Neal hugged me. Ed was relieved.

To anyone who has never soloed, the feeling is inexplicable. The feelings of accomplishment and joy were overwhelming. My face seemed welded into a permanent grin and, at the end of the day, ached because I couldn't keep from smiling.

Studying for the required written exam to obtain a license was a breeze. Each night I would rush through dinner, and then reach for the books while Neal did the dishes. My mind was riveted to principles of flight, mechanics of an aircraft, FAA regulations, navigation and weather. By Thanksgiving I had passed the written exam. The desire to learn everything in these books was compulsive. In fact, flying was compulsive. I ate it, breathed it, walked it, talked it, dreamed about it and bored the hell out of anybody who would stand still for a minute and listen to me babble on about how wonderful it was. Their eyes would glaze over and they would smile patiently.

Neal solidly supported my flying. He never questioned the money or the time spent in this venture. He praised me when the landings were good and gave me comfort when they weren't. When I despaired of ever learning all the complicated procedures and wanted to sell the plane and forget the whole thing, Neal paid no attention. He had taken four lessons from Ed and decided it was too tough for him. He could understand how overwhelming it could be. But he could also understand how much I loved the sky and would not let me quit if he could help it.

The FAA required certification of the hand controls. Blueprints were sent to the engineering department in Fort Worth. The FAA sent their engineer to Siloam Springs to inspect them and issue a document called a 337. All of this seemed tedious and time consuming.

I spent the next few months flying solo, along with a few more lessons on instrument flying, night flying and cross-country trips. Before long I was ready for the big one – the exam for the pilot's license. All the requirements were met and I was ready for the flight exam. Since I had a medical waiver on my medical certificate, a medical flight examiner at the GADO office in Little Rock had to give me the flight test. This was scary business. Siloam Springs was an uncontrolled airport, requiring very little radio communication. However, Adams Field at Little Rock had approach control, control tower and ground control. These radio communications had to be followed. The Skyhawk had an old Mark V radio, which could either communicate or navigate by a VOR, but could not do both at the same time. The solo flight to Little Rock was fun and I miraculously found Adams Field. Since I did not have my license yet, I could not carry passengers.

Neal flew with Ed in another plane to Little Rock. Neal and I checked into a motel and I went to bed early, anticipating the following demanding day. Sleep wouldn't come. The more I realized how important it was to get a good night's rest, the more awake I became. My eyelids seemed frozen wide open. Dawn finally came.

The flight examiner omitted nothing. For the first two hours he gave me problems on weights and balances, cross-country flight planning and other questions. Finally he said, "Let's go fly."

We started across the ramp to the plane. I stumbled on a rock and fell flat on my face. I felt like a fool. The examiner helped me up and courageously climbed into the plane with me anyway.

He watched me intently as I made each landing, each take-off and each of the many emergency procedures. The two hours and 20 minutes seemed like days. Since 1:00 p.m. had come and gone, I did suggest to him once that we were missing our lunch, hoping he would take the hint. Finally he suggested we return to Adams Field.

"Whew! It's finally over," I thought. I set the course for Little Rock and radioed approach control. In a few minutes they turned me over to the control tower and I was cleared to land on Runway 35. The final approach was fine, but I leveled off four feet above the runway. The examiner had to take over the controls and land the plane. I was heartsick and felt like crying. I knew I had failed the exam.

The examiner climbed out and said, "I'll meet you upstairs in a few minutes."

Neal walked over to the plane and asked, "How did it go?"

With a huge lump in my throat and on the verge of tears I said, "I didn't pass."

"Is he just leaving you here on the ramp?" Neal asked incredulously.

"No, he wants to talk to me," I answered, feeling heart-broken.

As we walked toward the office, I began to think of several prospects who might be interested in buying a Skyhawk, priced for a quick sale.

Sitting across from the examiner's desk, he told me some things on which I needed to practice. Then he said, "Donna, you're a safe pilot. We're giving you a license."

Several seconds passed before I realized what he had said. "You're just kidding me," I finally said.

No, he wasn't kidding. At that very moment I became a licensed single-engine, fixed-wing aircraft pilot. Relief, amazement, gratitude, disbelief! This hard-earned ticket was really mine. This emotionally charged moment was exquisitely beautiful. I now felt like weeping from the pure joy of it.

Neal could fly back to Siloam Springs with me now that I had the prized license. Twenty miles south of the airport I radioed, "N7724X, 20 miles south inbound for landing. And by the way, I have a passenger." The guys at the airport knew I had gone to Little Rock for check-ride. They also knew that if I had a passenger I had passed. They cheered me home.

CHAPTER 18

We can all handle "what is."

We had flown to Hot Springs on Friday afternoon, the first week in August, 1973, for the annual AA Convention. As soon as the last meeting was over, we took a cab to the Hot Springs Airport. The temperature was a sweltering 100 degrees and the still air was loaded with an oppressive haze. The weather briefing indicated scattered clouds at 3000 feet and four miles visibility, a typical August afternoon. Climbing to 8500 feet after take-off, the temperature gradually decreased about four degrees for every 1000 feet. We leveled off in the cool 68-degree temperature and sat back to enjoy the puffy white cumulous clouds surrounding us.

Suddenly the engine sputtered, coughed, then sputtered again. "What's going on?" Neal gasped.

I quickly pulled the carburetor heat (to melt ice that may have accumulated in the tubing carrying fuel to the engine), and followed the emergency checklist. My hands were trembling and my heart was beating so fast I could hardly breathe. I radioed the Hot Springs Control Tower and told them we had an emergency. "It looks like the engine is failing!" Neal was pumping the throttle, but the altimeter was quickly unwinding – 8400, 8300, 8200. Pumping the throttle seemed to be the only thing keeping the engine running at all.

"N7724X, what is your position from Little Rock?" the Hot Springs Tower asked.

"24X is 274 degrees off Little Rock," my shaky voice replied.

"24X, you are 20 miles northwest of Hot Springs," they advised.

The altimeter now read 5000 feet. That's above sea level. The mountains under us rose to 2800 feet above sea level. We had 2200 feet of space between the tree covered ground and our tiny aircraft. Descending at 500 feet per minute (glide speed) and an airspeed of 80 miles an hour, 20 miles would take 15 minutes. But we only had 4 minutes and 24 seconds before … I also knew that beneath the scattered clouds lay a blanket of haze, and then trees, trees, and more trees. No road. No highways. No pastures. Nothing but trees.

"Hot Springs Tower, 24X will never make it."

The tower cleared all other air traffic to another frequency, alerted the rescue units and stayed with 24X. From the trembling in my voice, they knew I was really scared. Meanwhile, Neal's pumping the throttle seemed to be leveling the engine out. Power was returning spasmodically. The prop was turning faster. Just before we slipped into the clouds, the engine started running smoothly. We kept the tower informed of our progress. The tower told us to climb back to 7500 if possible. The calm voice on the radio advised me, "The sky is mostly overcast, but there's a hole in the clouds just northwest of the airport. Stay at level 7500 if you can, until you have the airport in sight."

Seconds seemed like hours. We had just experienced a potentially fatal situation. We were scared, but was it fear of dying? Probably. We were so busy doing the right things that imminent death was not a conscious thought.

Our eyes searched for a glimpse of the airport. Then we saw it.

"There it is!" we screamed. "24X has the field in sight!" I radioed.

"24X is cleared to land," the tower advised. "And I bet that's the prettiest sight you've seen all day! Give us a call when you get on the ground."

We spiraled down from 7500 feet, swung left to enter final approach, landed and taxied to the ramp.

"What do you think happened?" the controller asked.

"There are three possibilities," I replied. "The first and most likely cause of our problem was carburetor ice, especially on such a hot, humid day. The second possibility could have been debris in the fuel line, and thirdly, Cessna 172s are susceptible to vapor locking at altitudes above 5000 feet."

The mechanics checked the plane carefully. Everything was in perfect order. They could find nothing wrong. After a sandwich from the airport restaurant, we climbed back into the plane. The trip back home was comparatively dull.

CHAPTER 19

Fear is wanting to be safe.
Safety is an illusion.

Just for the fun if it, I took a real estate course by correspondence from the University of Arkansas. The material was terribly dull. However, once I started I felt duty bound to finish it. After I passed the final, I thought that while the material was still fresh in my mind, it would be a good time to take the state broker's exam. Since the exam was only given in Little Rock, this gave me a good excuse to fly. Even though I had never darkened the door of a real estate office, I passed the test and was given a broker's license anyway.

Our next-door neighbor, Walter Gray, owned the best agency in town. When he learned I was taking the course, he told me, "I have a desk and office waiting for you when you're ready to start selling real estate."

It would be a bit of a gamble, though. The cost of keeping an airplane was astronomical. The salary at the Medical Center along with Neal's salary at City Hall was paying the bills. Would I be able to sell enough to bring in some income? I had never sold a piece of property in my whole life. I might not even like selling any more than I liked being a technician. "Oh, well, I'll never know unless I try it," I thought. So, I quit the boring and dreary job at the medical center.

Of course I didn't know how to sell. I hung around the office, attended the sales meetings and started acquainting myself with the listings. I joined the sales force on the tours to see new listings. For the first time in 18 years I was working with physically healthy people … a healthy change for me.

Weeks went by without a sale, or even a client to whom I could show property. Then one July morning in 1972 some people came in and I was the only sales person available. I told them they were my first clients, which helped to relieve some of my anxiety. Fumbling through the qualifying process they were very patient with me. Finally we all left my office to look at some listings that fit their needs. Unbelievably, they liked the first place I showed them and wanted to buy it. I was so stunned I could hardly write up the sales contract. A couple of times I didn't know how to fill in some of the blanks. Walter helped me. In several weeks I received my first commission check. "Hmmmm," I thought, "this might turn out to be a better deal than I thought." I started taking my work more seriously.

All of the sales people rotated the days they were scheduled to be "up." This meant they were responsible for walk-in clients. It was my day "up" when a couple from Wichita, Joe and Mary, wanted to look at 90 wooded acres on the Illinois River. We could only look at part of it because many areas were unreachable by car. On the way back to town I asked, "Would you like to see that 90 acres from the air?"

What could they say? There were captive in my car! "Of course," they said.

We stopped at the airport and I pulled the plane from the hangar.

I caught Joe cutting his eyes at me, silently asking, amazed, "Is she the pilot? What have we gotten ourselves into?"

"Let's go," I called.

They were good sports and climbed into the plane. The winding Arkansas River and the towering pines looked beautiful from the air. We circled and circled until the property lines were clearly defined. We landed back at the airport and taxied up to the ramp. I heard Joe mumble, "I don't believe this."

Joe and Mary bought the property.

Walter sent me to Tulsa one fall day to pick up a client arriving from California. Tulsa International Airport had a parking place for small planes located close to the arriving gates. I taxied to this area, parked the plane and walked to the gate to wait for the client. When he came I introduced myself and we walked to the exit. "How far is it to Siloam Springs?" he asked.

"About 90 miles," I answered. "We can be there in 30 minutes."

He looked at me strangely. I directed him to the plane. It was then he realized what was going on.

"Do you mind flying in a small plane?" I asked, unlocking the right door for him. What could he say?

The trip could not have been more beautiful. The fall leaves were red, orange, yellow, maroon and sprinkled with a thousand hues of combined colors. The tall green pines provided a background for this spectacular display. We flew low, soaking in the rich colors. He hardly noticed the pilot wore artificial legs and used hand controls to fly the plane.

My co-workers lovingly called me their corporate pilot. I flew their clients over farms and ranches. Sometimes I flew to distant places for closings on real estate contracts. I LOVED IT!!

CHAPTER 20

Depression is another word for self-pity.

As long as I could do things to keep distracted, I could ignore the growing sense of hopelessness and despair inside of me. I had fun at the real estate office or when I was flying. But home alone with Neal was becoming increasingly difficult. The feeling of being trapped lay just beneath the surface. I covered it with a smile and a positive attitude so that outwardly everything looked fine. We went to AA meetings together, entertained many friends and flew to conventions and meetings all over the country. At many of these meetings both Neal and I were speakers. It would seem that we adored each other and life could not be better.

But I couldn't stand for Neal to touch me.

At night before going to sleep, I felt hopeless, just on the edge of crying. The effort to put on the happy face and pretend everything was lovely when it was not drained my energy. Fatigue was my constant companion. There was uneasiness just under the surface, a feeling of something not quite right.

"Surely there must be something wrong with me." I concluded.

I was reading all the self-help books I could lay my hands on. I had gone to the Christian church for years, hoping to find some answers. Neal was a member of the First Christian Church and I had given it my best shot. We went to church on Sunday morning and night and prayer meeting on Wednesday. I just couldn't choke down what they were teaching. Then Neal and I became involved in the Unity church. In fact, we had flown to Unity village near Kansas City several times on Sunday morning to services. The Unity teachings seemed a bit easier for me to swallow.

Finally, in 1975 I reached out to a counselor. I told him how I felt about Neal.

He said, "Donna, feeling the way you do, you have two choices. You can wait around until he dies or you can get a divorce. As your friend and counselor, I'm advising you to leave the marriage."

Leave the marriage? That was not what I wanted to hear. That had not been an option. It had just never occurred to me to get a divorce. "I can't do that," I sobbed. "I don't have a reason to leave."

"As strongly as you feel, you don't need a reason," he replied.

Desperate, I said, "I want you to tell me how to change my attitude so I can stay in the marriage."

He had no answer.

The next few years became progressively more difficult. Neal's retirement only accentuated the problem since he was always home. He seemed to love me, which made it more difficult. He never put me down or made me feel stupid. He was supportive in everything I did, complimented me on every meal, liked everything I bought and admired everything I wore.

Why would I feel all this aversion to him? I was married to a charming, kind, thoughtful husband, but I didn't want to live with him. I tried everything to change how I felt. I read theology and philosophy books. Surely the great writers and religious teachers had some clues about how to have peace and joy and serenity, regardless of the circumstances. I concentrated on working with others in my 12-step program. The eleventh step in the program suggested, "Sought through prayer and meditation to improve our conscious contact with God as we understand him." Hmmm. Maybe some work in that area would helpful. Belief in God seemed to be a running thread in all the books. Again, the 12-step program suggested, "letting go and letting God" or "turning your life and will over to the care of God." I tried all of that over and over. At times it seemed to work. The 12-step program came the closest to working. The results were visible in those who worked the program. Their lives reflected an inner change of some sort that couldn't be understood or denied. I worked the steps to the best of my ability, but ultimately I would end up hopeless and depressed. Was there any system or creed or information that would work consistently?

"Maybe I just need to grow up," I thought. "Am I missing something that would allow me to live in peace, regardless of the circumstances and people around me? Or is life just a blend of heartache and happiness and all I have to do is grit my teeth, take the bitter with the better, and maybe I can make it. Make it to what? What was it that keeps me from being happy – Right Now?"

I had all the creature comforts. What am I whining about? The questions were endless and tiresome. There had to be more to life than making a living, having a relationship, paying off debts, building a dream house, or buying new clothes or a new car. "Is that all there is?" I wondered. The last desperate words each night before sleep came were: "God help me."

In 1979 a dear friend invited me to come to Whitney, Texas, for the weekend. The flight to Texas was a routine one. I had flown my airplane into the Whitney State Park air strip many times to attend seminars held in a special chapel. The round building was called the Chapel of Light. The lower floor was used for office space, a lounge, kitchen and restrooms. The upper level provided a meeting place, a sanctuary, surrounded by 13 large windows. Each window reflected a different hue of rainbow colors. People came from all parts of the country to enjoy the peace that always seemed to be present. The chapel was the result of a dream in 1971 by my long-time friend Marce White. It was not something she wanted to build, but the impressions were so strong that she shared the dream with a few close friends. They supported her and the project was soon started. To raise money for the construction, monthly seminars were offered that included teaching spiritual truths, which avoided all denominational creeds and doctrines. Since I was searching, searching, searching, I was pulled to Whitney many times. Friends met me at the airport and took me to their home for the weekend. After one Saturday morning session, Marce invited me to lunch. Sitting on her deck overlooking Lake Whitney, Marce said, "We're looking for a coordinator for the Chapel."

Without thinking, I said, "Where do I apply?"

We talked about what the duties and responsibilities of a coordinator would be. Marce explained that I would be running the book store, setting up weekend seminars, arranging Sunday services, inviting speakers, keeping track of the money, making financial reports, writing and sending out a monthly newsletter and working with the 12-member board of trustees.

I wanted the job. Maybe some of my uneasiness would be resolved in this spiritual atmosphere. I was willing to take some drastic steps to find some peace.

When I got home to Siloam Springs, I told Neal about the conversation with Marce. Neal was ready to go to Whitney. He had retired from the city office three years earlier and living on the lake seemed like a wonderful idea. In fact, he was convinced we needed to move to Whitney and would not listen to me when I wavered about moving there. I wasn't sure about coordinating all of the activities at the Chapel. In my state of mind it wasn't likely I could handle it. However, the Board of Trustees thought I could do it and hired me.

We leased our home, called a moving company, packed the cars and headed for Texas. We couldn't fly the plane to Texas. The large, steel hangar door had slipped from its track, skinning the leading edge of the wing. The plane was in the shop for repairs.

One of the chapel friends let us live in their rental home until we decided to build or buy a house. Half of our furniture was put in storage because the rental house was so small. The wonderful conveniences of a garbage disposal, central heat and air, storage space and two bathrooms were things of the past. Adapting to these changes took its toll. There was no room to be alone. Neal was always there. On my day off, I wanted to run away from home.

"What in the hell is wrong with me?" I cried.

I listened intently to the chapel speakers, read hundreds of books, meditated, and earnestly sought the answer to my feelings of being trapped. Depression hovered over me like a dark cloud. There seemed to be no answer.

On Friday, October 10, 1979, I came home to find Neal sitting on the couch, struggling for each breath. "What's wrong?" I cried out, sensing that something terrible had happened. "I had a sharp pain in my chest this morning and I've had trouble breathing ever since," he gasped.

"Let's go to the doctor," I pleaded.

"No, he replied. "If I'm not better by morning, I'll go then." He was not better. He was worse. Unable to breathe lying down, he sat up all night. His discomfort was so intense that sleep was impossible.

Saturday morning at the clinic, the doctor believed Neal's emphysema was causing the shortness of breath. He gave him some medicine and sent him home, but the medicine brought no relief. Neal had another sleepless, breathless, miserable night. I knew he was going to die if he didn't get some help. On Sunday, I called the doctor and he said to take Neal to the hospital. The x-rays revealed a collapsed lung. They rushed him to the emergency room and inserted a tube through his ribs to re-inflate his lung. He was in the hospital for six days.

I felt scared and very guilty. I had not been the easiest person to live with lately. I regretted being so touchy and irritable with him. What if he had died? I would have carried a load of guilt around for a long time. After he came home to recover, I tried harder to let him know I loved him. But did I love him? Something was terribly wrong and it had to be something wrong with me.

Neal seemed to be doing well, so three friends. Elwin, Marce, Sherry and I traveled to Austin to attend a lecture by a speaker we wanted to hear. We were all part of the chapel group and were always looking for new speakers we could invite to the chapel for a seminar or weekend workshop.

Before leaving the motel the next morning, I suddenly stumbled backward and fell on my left hip. I tried to stand up, but couldn't. I took my artificial legs off and tried to stand and walk. I couldn't. The pain was so severe that I couldn't move. My friends filled the tub with hot water and helped me into it, hoping that soaking would relieve the pain. It didn't. I had fallen hundreds of times and had never hurt myself.

"Surely the pain will go away shortly," I reassured them through gritted teeth.

If I sat real still, there was no pain. So I put my legs back on very carefully. The bellboy carried me to the car and we started the 140-mile trip back to Whitney. All of us were so hungry that by the time we were on the road, we decided to stop at the Stagecoach Inn in Salado for lunch. I thought by this time the pain would be gone. Wrong. The moment I tried to stand, the pain was incredible.

The only way I could get into the restaurant was on my hands and wooden knees. I crawled to the entrance, up the steps and through the door, feeling ridiculous and silly. I had to go to the bathroom immediately, so I crawled to the bathroom and pulled myself onto the toilet seat. "What a relief! I made it!" But the dining room seemed five miles away. I didn't need to worry. My creative friends brought a high chair on rollers to the restroom, helped me onto it and wheeled me to a table.

The dinner was outstanding. When we were ready to leave, two men carried me to the car. Elwin insisted we stop by Scott & White Hospital and see a doctor. The x-rays showed no broken bones. Of course, I couldn't break a hip since I didn't have any. However, the muscles, ligaments and tendons were injured and would take time to heal.

During this healing time, with or without legs, I was nearly helpless. I didn't like it. Everywhere I went, even at the chapel, I had to ask somebody to carry me. This crazy accident reminded me, again, how loving and helpful people want to be when given a chance. I found my old aluminum armband crutches and started using them again. Little by little I recovered. Just in time to attend Daddy's funeral.

CHAPTER 21

There is nothing to be regretful about.
There is nothing to be ashamed about.

Two years after Mother died, Daddy had remarried. Everyone loved Gladys, his new wife. Gladys, Mother and Daddy had gone to high school together and had been friends for years. Daddy had retired from the gasoline business in 1954. He bought 230 acres of land south of town. Part of the land was in pasture which he put cattle on. Seventy acres were in wheat. Daddy and Gladys loved to fish on the three ponds.

They had many good times, loved to go dancing and play cards. On Christmas Day, 1975, Gladys died suddenly from a heart attack. Without Gladys, the loneliness and pain were more than Daddy could bear. Alcohol was the only thing that would ease the pain and let him sleep. He felt useless. At 75 he thought he was too old to find a purpose for living. Depression was his constant companion. I would fly to South Haven to see him at least once a month.

"What do I have to live for?" Daddy would ask me.

I had no answers for him. I was asking myself the same questions. There had to be more to life than money, cars, and dream homes. But what?

"Where is the joy of living? What is it that makes life worthwhile?" The questions played over and over in my mind.

All I could do for Daddy was to thank him for the life Mother and him had given me. They had allowed me to have the freedom to manage my own life without interference, suggestions or judgment. What an incredible gift they had given me!

On April 2, 1980, my brother Delbert called me at the chapel. Daddy was dead. We would never know if his death was an accident or intentional. He had gone to the farm that morning to feed the cattle. Delbert had seen him around noon and noticed he had been drinking. The next morning Delbert called and there was no answer. He went to the house to check on him. Delbert pulled the garage door up. He was in the car. The death certificate said, "Carbon monoxide poisoning."

I was really okay with his death. I knew my Daddy had done the best he could do with the light he had to see by. He could not have done it differently. If he could have done it differently, he would have. He had been miserable for a long time.

Daddy had probably made the smart decision. Life was "the pits" so he checked out. These thoughts kept running around in my head. Then I would feel guilty because I had hundreds of reasons to feel grateful. I listed them, kept a journal and tried to feel grateful, yet, inevitably, "So what?" was my conclusion. Life was a tremendously heavy burden. I was too tired to live it and knew no way out. I felt trapped. Emerson was probably right: *"Most men live out their lives in quiet desperation."*

In the midst of this gloom there was one bright spot. With the money from the sale of our home in Arkansas and a small inheritance from Daddy's estate, we built a new home. The furniture we had stored when we first moved to Whitney was set in place. The extra space was heavenly. The view from the deck overlooking Lake Whitney was breathtaking. This view provided some peace and solace for both Neal and me.

CHAPTER 22

We lie to be safe.

June 28, 1981, I came home from work to find Neal lying on the deck lounge chair, exhausted.

"What's happened?" I asked, terrified.

"I don't know," he replied. "It seemed that someone else was in control of my mind."

"Where's the car? And our poodle, Molly?" I gasped, realizing that something was terribly wrong. I had given the adorable poodle to Neal for Christmas, 1976. He fell in love with her immediately.

Shaking his head in confusion, "Let's go see if we can find Molly and the car," he mumbled.

Little by little we pieced the situation together. Neal had left the house that morning to go to the post office. He had a golf game scheduled at 10:00 a.m. He never made it to the golf course. Instead he headed for the lake on roads he had never traveled before, driving 100 miles per hour. He turned down one road that led to the lake and drove the car right into the water where the engine died about 30 feet from dry ground. He was disoriented and sweltering in the 100 degree temperature. Somehow he found his way, walking the four miles home.

We drove and looked and looked and drove. No car. No Molly. In desperation we drove over to our friend Joe's house for help. He just happened to be on vacation that week so we found him home. After listening to Neal's description of his wild ride, Joe, who had been duck hunting in that area the previous season, led us right to the car. We called and called for Molly. Molly was nowhere to be found. We feared she must have tried to swim from the car and had drowned. After the wrecker pulled the car to town, we returned to the lake and miraculously found a dirty, tired and wet poodle.

Still confused and disoriented Neal went to the bathroom to take a shower. I sat in the chair, stunned by these shockers. Five minutes, ten minutes, 15 minutes passed and the shower was still running. I hurried to the bathroom to check on him. The shower was going but Neal was gone. The shower was empty. I found him on the bed with his clothes on, soaking wet, asleep.

Confused and frightened I felt helpless and alone. I checked every few minutes to see if he was still breathing. Something terrible was happening to him. My mind created all sorts of insane projections. The night seemed endless.

The next morning the doctor diagnosed Neal's condition as a stroke and recommended he rest and not drive. The following week was filled with madness. Neal was terrified, confused and his behavior was crazy. He carried on long conversations with imaginary people. When he thought he was appropriately dressed, he had failed to put on shoes and socks. He smoked imaginary cigarettes and ate his food with his hands. It seemed that all the connections in his brain were short-circuited. Watching all this insanity, I felt so sad and so sorry for him. Even today as I sit here typing this, my eyes fill with tears remembering the turmoil and distress he was experiencing. There seemed to be nothing I could do but watch and be patient with him. This was easy to do because I knew he could not help what was going on or what was happening. The hard part was to stand by and watch him struggle for a sense of reality. I could not do it for him.

Slowly and gradually his behavior improved. The doctor allowed him to drive short distances. So, he did the grocery shopping, went to AA meetings and appeared somewhat normal again. Somewhat normal was all. Neal was drinking his coffee at the food bar early one morning in the kitchen. On my way into the room I heard Neal desperately mumble, "I must be losing my mind." The pain of seeing him in this condition was almost impossible to endure.

A few weeks after his "car in the lake" episode, the cleaning lady quit because Neal had made sexual advances toward her, exposing himself. I did not take these episodes very seriously because I felt they were happening as the result of his stroke and knew he was totally harmless.

I talked to Neal about this behavior. I told him to not feel guilty about it. It was just part of his sickness. He promised it would never happen again.

But it did.

Neal had gone to an AA meeting that Monday night. The phone rang shortly after he had left. It was the new cleaning woman's husband. He was totally enraged that Neal would do such an unspeakable thing to his wife. Neal had, once again, exposed himself to her. I tried to calm the husband down, explaining that Neal was sick and harmless. He would not hear anything I had to say, ending the conversation by slamming down the phone. When Neal walked in around 9:00 p.m, I was sitting at the food bar. He sat down across from me.

I quietly said, "It's happened again."

"What's happened?" he asked.

I told him about the phone call. He denied it and abruptly marched upstairs. I followed him. Confused and shaken, I searched for words.

Finally, on the verge of tears, I sobbed, "I can't keep from crying."

"I've cried all my life," Neal replied, sadly, biting his lower lip to keep from crying. "I thought the AA program would take care of it. But it didn't."

I didn't know what he was talking about. In desperation I suggested, "We need help. Please call Dr. Hill in the morning. Maybe he can refer us to a psychiatrist." Dr. Hill recommended a psychiatrist in Waco. The following day Neal drove to Waco for a consultation. When he returned home he told me that Dr. Winter wanted to talk to me.

"He also wants me to go to the hospital for some tests. He has made arrangements for me to be admitted on Friday."

"I'll do anything. Something is terribly wrong and we need somebody to help us," I said hopefully,

The ride to Waco on Friday to see the doctor was grim. There were no words. Each of us seemed to be in our own world of uncertainty and upheaval. The future was unthinkable.

When I sat down in Dr. Winter's office, his first words were, "Mr. Lancaster is very smooth."

A bit surprised by this comment, I nodded cautiously.

He continued, "Neal's problem began long before you met him. Neal is a child molester."

Shock was followed by rage. I felt enraged, used, abused and deceived. Images and impressions from the past flooded my thoughts. The doctor said nothing while I experienced these powerful emotions. Then slowly the picture came into view. It was like there was a huge picture puzzle of our lives on the wall, only there was one piece missing. Dr. Winter had put the missing piece in place. I could see and remember and knew; I knew he was telling the truth. I remembered the time I saw Neal and the 12-year-old daughter of friends in Neal's car. The 12-year-old was driving. At that time, pain went through every cell of my body like an atomic blast. I dismissed it as jealously on my part. In my naiveté, it never occurred to me that something very sick was going on.

Now I knew.

"I don't know if I can stay in the marriage. Can Neal make it alone?"

"We'll have to see. I'll help him all I can," Dr. Winter advised.

At the hospital I helped Neal check in and unpack. His home for the next two weeks would be the psychiatric floor of Providence Hospital. Locked in.

On my way home I started sorting things out.

So that was it. Now I understood why our marriage could be nothing less than perfect. Neal knew and had always known that if we had bumpy places in our relationship, he would have to look at the one thing he could not bear to look at. It was so despicable, so awful to him that he could not reveal it, not even in the many self-searching inventories the AA program had suggested. We both played the role of "everything is wonderful" and put on the façade, unwilling to admit that our marriage was not perfect. Both of us were dying. It was not Neal who caused my unhappiness. It was my inability to be open and honest about how I felt. I just couldn't do it. The risk was too great. What risk? Rejection? Disapproval? What would people think? All of this seemed ridiculous and insane now.

Now, with this new information there was a different twist. I had looked for years for a justification to leave the marriage. I could now leave and not feel guilty. The very thought of it exhilarated me. But what about Neal? It seemed that he was almost a non-entity at this point. To feel sorry for him would not make him well. It would only make me sick, pulling me into his nightmare. Although I knew that he could not help doing the things he was doing, I also knew there was no treatment. His body was healthy and the future with him seemed full of torment. I reasoned that I was not responsible for him. He was an adult. I did not realize at this point that the tests from the hospital would reveal that he suffered from atrophy of the brain. He was mentally incapable of taking care of himself.

Once the decision was made to get a divorce, it was irreversible. Tons of weight seemed to fall away and I felt a lightness and enthusiasm for living for the first time in many, many years.

I spent the weekend looking at the facts and assimilating the shocking information. I drove to Providence Hospital on Monday morning. I was ushered through the locked doors into a small waiting room. The nurses escorted Neal to the visitors' area. He appeared disheveled and confused.

"I'm on my way to an attorney to file for divorce," I said quietly.

"I don't blame you," he replied.

"I've written down a financial settlement, splitting everything right down the middle. My inheritance from Daddy paid for our house and was not subject to the settlement. We have $20,000 in savings from the sale of the plane. You'll also receive the mortgage payments from the house in Arkansas. These payments, plus your Social Security will give you over $1,000 a month. Look this over and see if it's all right with you." I handed him a piece of paper with the figures. "I love you and I'm grateful for our life together. I'm sorry for all the mistakes I've made and for all the times I've hurt you. I love you but I can't live with you any longer. I'll do everything I can to help you adjust to living alone."

Before we could have any more discussion, a nurse came to take Neal for some x-rays. This ended the conversation.

I filed for divorce on October 5, 1981. During the next few weeks I found a place for Neal to live and packed his belongings. When he left the hospital his new home was ready. He had enough income to live on, a car to drive and Molly. I either saw him daily when we went to meetings or talked to him on the phone. Each time I assured him he could make it. He never complained or objected. He seemed in a complete state of non-resistance. Perhaps the whole process of uncovering his dark secret was too much for him. Life was more than he could bear.

The AA and Al-Anon communities were appalled. When someone would ask me, "Why a divorce?"

"It's just what I have to do." I answered. I was not going to air his problem to others. It was none of their business. I also didn't want to hurt Neal anymore. I really wanted him to be whole and healthy. I was blind to the fact that his brain atrophy made wholeness impossible for him. I was not aware of that information until after I had filed for divorce. At that point it seemed too late to change the direction events were propelling me. The moment had come and gone. There was no turning back

On December 14, 1981, the divorce was final. We were so friendly and cooperative with each other, the attorney questioned why we were even getting a divorce. I didn't, or couldn't go into that issue. It was too painful for both of us. Since we were no longer married, we had new wills prepared, which we signed immediately after the divorce decree. Neal left his estate to me. I left my estate to Neal. We both added a cremation clause.

It was as simple as that.

CHAPTER 23

The only time we want to change anything is when we think we know the future.

A week before Christmas I invited Neal to eat Christmas dinner with me and some friends from the chapel. He said he had made plans to visit his brother, John and his wife, Polly, in Ponca City, Oklahoma. Everyone who knew about his plans wanted him to take a bus, but he insisted on driving the 350 miles. The morning he left he came by the chapel where I was working. We spread out the road map and planned his trip. As he walked out the door, I handed him the map, which he had forgotten to pick up.

He turned and said, "I don't need a map. All I need is God."

He looked so lost and alone, it was all I could do to keep from going with him. I would punish myself many times later because I had let him go knowing he was in no condition to make the trip alone. He made a wrong turn in Fort Worth and ended up in Cisco, 200 miles in the wrong direction. His car had broken down or who knows where he would have ended up. He called me from a motel. We decided to leave the car in Cisco at a garage to be repaired and he would take the bus on to Ponca City. I called Polly and told her what had happened. She said she would call me when Neal arrived. I heard nothing from her all night. Finally she called. Neal had arrived the night before, disoriented, unshaven, confused and lost. John and Polly were angry with me for allowing Neal to leave Whitney in such an unstable state.

While he was there, Neal told John and Polly that he had made it clear in his will that he should be cremated after his death. For some reason, known only to him, he felt the need to deliver this information to his family and he was the only one who could do it.

A few days later he began his trip back to Whitney by bus. He was still disoriented and felt he could not stay on the bus. In Oklahoma City he got off and called me to find someone to come and get him. I did. Jim and Betty lived near Neal. They had been checking on him every day. Jim agreed to drive to Oklahoma City and bring him home.

Throughout the Christmas holidays I felt touchy and irritable. Loud noises made me want to scream. I couldn't keep from crying. Something terrible was happening.

Two weeks had passed since the divorce was final.

On Sunday morning, January 3, 1982, Jim stepped into my office after the chapel service.

"Donna," he said softly, "Betty and I stopped by to check on Neal this morning. Apparently he died in his sleep."

"NO! NO! NO! He can't die. He's going to make it!" The pain was unbearable. Guilt. Anger. Sorrow. Grief. Self-condemnation. Emptiness. These emotions flooded over me. The only relief came from weeping.

The director of the funeral home needed someone to advise him concerning the services. There was no one else to take care of arrangements except me. Legally, I was Neal's ex-wife. Emotionally, I was his widow. I showed the director Neal's will, which included his instructions to cremate his body. However, I was not Neal's wife and I could not sign the necessary papers. The director called John, Neal's brother, to confirm the written instructions. Neal had made it to Ponca City and told them his request. Just in time.

Neal's daughter, Lisa, and her fiancé arrived early Monday morning in time for the memorial service on Tuesday. Lisa and I shared the information that had been hidden for a long time. Lisa had known for many years about her father's problem. He had never touched her, although her stepsisters were still going to counselors regarding their problems related to Neal molesting them.

John and Polly, Katherine, Delbert and Donna came to Whitney for the service. The memorial service was held at the chapel. The AA community all attended. Even though they didn't know what was going on, they continued to love Neal and me. Neal had made an incredible contribution to the lives of hundreds of alcoholics and their families in Whitney, as well as in Siloam Springs. Everyone remembered Neal as loving, considerate and full of fun and laughter. The service was a celebration of his life. The whole family was comforted.

John, Polly and Katherine were still angry, which was understandable. They felt like I had abandoned Neal, took all the money and left him to die. I was so emotionally raw that it was hard for me to ignore these suggestions. When I called them, they let me know in no uncertain terms they did not want to communicate with me in any way. Many years later, after John had died, I made a trip to Ponca City and told Polly the whole story.

She said, "I knew there had to be more to it. I'm glad John is gone and never knew."

My greatest comfort came from a surprising source, Elise Lancaster, Neal's ex-wife and Lisa's mother.

Lisa and her mother had moved to Providence, Rhode Island, in the early 1960s. Elise was a skilled violinist and taught music. Lisa had been studying cello since early childhood. She applied and was accepted by the Julliard School of Music. She obtained her master's degree on scholarships and played with a prestigious New England string quartet. She continued to be a gifted and enthusiastic artist even after her marriage to Jeff.

Elise wrote me a letter. She and Neal were married in 1952. She had two daughters, Lisa's stepsisters, whom Neal had molested. They were divorced in 1956 for obvious reasons. Twenty-five years had gone by, yet she took the time to write me the following:

Dear Donna,

I just had a long, long phone conversation with Lisa and it left me so moved at what had happened to you – to all of us – through Neal. I had to contact you and tell you that I am glad you are reexamining the whole thing and that I admire you for the way you tried in the way you knew best to support Neal to the end. I feel guilty because I could not.

I think Neal was one of the truly good people under terrible compulsions. God alone can imagine their horrible sources. I feel that Lisa is right and that he has been able to shed some of this with the severing of his body. Who knows? I trust her psychic instincts.

I'm sure you are going through a great deal of suffering and questioning. And right now, it's hard to see that that is good. But knowing you, I'm sure you will come out with gold. Do not worry about people who cannot understand. They are hurt. They could not believe what is really true if they heard. I am sorry they have hurt you. They are afraid.

Donna, if there is anything I can do for you, I would be only too happy.

I am glad that you are questioning everything. We all are. It is a very big question and sometimes I think those that seem the surest, know the least.

My best regards, Elise

Elise was the one person in the whole world (except maybe the psychiatrist) who knew the whole, ugly story. The letter was like a soothing balm on shattered and raw emotions. I read and re-read the letter, hungry to soak up the love, understanding and compassion Elise had offered me. I had no words to express the tremendous gratitude I felt for her.

CHAPTER 24

Life is intent on waking us up.

Guilt still enfolded me like a shroud. Memories crowded my mind, most of them sad and tragic. I remembered only the times when I had failed him, failed to listen and understand or failed to reach out and touch his hurting heart. I felt like I had deserted my best friend. In his own way, Neal was screaming for help. In my stubborn and self-serving way, I had stood there, unmoving, watching him fade away. The guilt was devastating.

My sick and battered emotions convinced me the divorce was a tragic mistake. Perhaps I had even killed him. I had prayed, meditated and lit candles. I had even been coordinator for the Chapel of Light for 2 years. That alone should have guided my life. God should have told me Neal was going to die. I would have stayed with him. I didn't want Neal to die. I wanted him to make it. *I knew* he would make it. But he didn't. Evidently there was no such thing as inner guidance. I had been betrayed into believing something that was not true. I was enraged.

Something happened that made me aware of my anger. Several friends and I were eating in a restaurant. A baby at the table next to us was crying. I remarked, "If that kid doesn't stop screaming, I'm going to kill it!" I had never been more certain of something. "WHOA!" I thought. This rage was something I had better deal with – now.

The moment I arrived home, I grabbed a pillow and found the tennis racket. With great gusto I began beating the pillow with every ounce of energy I had. I thought of everything and everybody I was or had been angry with and pictured their faces on the pillow and beat, beat, beat, saying all the mean, ugly things I had ever wanted to say. I screamed out everything I had bottled up for years. This went on for a long time. The more I beat, the more I remembered. I finally included myself in the tirade, berating myself for the mess I had made of my life and the self-hatred that was slowly destroying me. Then the big one: God had done it to me. So, with all the energy I would muster, I pictured God on the pillow and struck Him, over and over. With one crashing blow of the tennis racket, I killed Him.

It was over. I had probably never been this honest in my whole life. The God in the sky, the cosmic scorekeeper was dead, gone. Evidently there was no one to answer my prayers, give comfort, or give any indication that life was a worthwhile adventure. Any concepts of God, life, joy, life-everlasting, were shattered. I stood alone. There never had been, nor was there now, anyone up there who rewarded me when I was good or punished me when I was bad. There was no one out there to answer my pleas for help. Suddenly an overwhelming sense of peace and freedom enfolded me.

The old rigid belief system that had held me in bondage had crumbled. My ego wanted to live in a safe harbor, so I had believed things to be true, about God, Jesus, the Bible, without checking them out for myself. "It's better to be safe," the ego told me (even though it's not true) "than to stand naked and alone." But the price had become too high. I could no longer pretend I believed that which I could not believe. At this point I knew nothing, believed nothing. All my preconceived opinions had vanished like the illusions they really were. I felt a sense of joy that was indescribable. I knew nothing. I believed nothing. Life was one big joke. But the conflict was gone! The negative emotions were gone. Emptiness was a far more desirable inner state than deceit.

I was also responsible for my life. There was no one, including God, to blame if my life was not working or was a mess. The days of blaming others or events if I were happy, unhappy, sad, depressed or any of the other many states, were gone. I was totally responsible. Period. With this realization came great freedom. I didn't have to wait anymore for the world and/or the people in it to change in order for me to be happy.

CHAPTER 25

*We cannot control circumstances or how
other people treat us.
We can choose our responses to
circumstances and other people.*

The following months passed peacefully. I still didn't know anything other than I was alive. The past was gone, only an illusion in the recesses of my mind. The future was an unwritten page, waiting for me to write the daily script. The mind wanted to know the future so it could make arrangements to be comfortable and safe. Both the past and future are illusion because they are not now. This information seemed to simplify my life. The *now* was the only reality. My attention could be focused on this moment only, which removed much of the compulsive chatter going on in my head. The clamoring essentially stopped. The peace and silence were savored like raindrops in an arid desert.

In June I flew commercially to New York to visit an old friend, Betty, for a few days. Her home in Brooklyn Heights was close to everything. While Betty was at work, I hiked to the local grocery store without my tall legs. I strolled the promenade, a walkway that overlooked Manhattan, and visited with the people resting on the benches.

I wrote in my journal:

Betty left for work early this morning. We had discussed the groceries we needed for our evening meal. I wanted to do the shopping because she would come home tired, hungry and late. I had planned to use my crutches to go to the store, yet to carry a sack of groceries and walk at the same time was very difficult. I heard a conversation start in my head: you can carry the groceries without your legs on, so don't wear them. Besides, who cares, but you?

These thoughts made my heart pound. Could I really face the world outside again as a short person? I knew that someday I'd have to resolve this issue. I knew that as I aged the weight of the legs would physically take a toll on my body. But today? I broke out in a sweat as that decision dominated my thoughts. If not today, when? The fear was uncanny. What was the fear all about? Rejection? Disapproval? Inferiority? Shame? Discomfort? The time had come for me to look more carefully at the fear.

Dressed in my size one moccasins, slacks for my little legs and my favorite blue sweatshirt, I opened the door of Betty's home and stepped into the outside world. The door clicking shut behind me sounded like a train accident. A wave of fear hit me, then passed. I had to tilt my head upward to smile and speak to everyone I met, and friendly eyes spoke back to me. A few people would not consent to eye contact, but I didn't take it personally. They were probably wrapped up in their stuff, not mine.

I skipped the two blocks to the grocery store and pushed the shopping cart through the aisles, the handle of the cart above my head. I asked clerks or other shoppers to hand me the items I couldn't reach. I was surprised how eager they were to help me. I absorbed the warmth and friendliness of these strangers. It seemed the cocoon of self-absorption and self-concern I had lived in for so long was breaking away. I was allowing myself to feel the outside world and I was finding it to be a very loving and gentle place.

I was beginning to see that soon I would set the legs aside. The legs were heavy and cumbersome and limited my physical freedom. I had no idea how difficult that would be.

On the way to Whitney from DFW Airport, I stopped at the Cleburne Municipal Airport, 35 miles north of Whitney, to see my friends Sam and Betty Ball. They operated the airport and were helpful when I had my plane tied down on their ramp. During the visit, Sam told me that he was looking for someone to do some of the office paperwork and shop billing. I was immediately interested. It sounded like a lot more fun to be around planes and pilots than to set up boring seminars and Sunday services.

"I'd like to apply for the job," I told Sam.

"I can't pay very much," Sam countered. "I can only pay $5 an hour. I'm sure you make more than that now."

"I don't care. If you'll hire me and teach me what I need to know, I want the job." I earnestly pleaded.

"You've got it," Sam smiled. "When can you start?"

"I'll turn in my resignation tomorrow and give them a month to find someone to replace me. How about July 15?"

That was fine with him.

"WOW! I get to work at an airport. I get to work in the magic world of aviation! What an opportunity!" I sang all the way home.

Sam was a patient teacher. I discovered he didn't like to do shop billing; sending our statements to the owners for labor and parts on their aircraft. Sam was a year behind, amounting to thousands of dollars. The mechanics would write their hours on their time cards for each job. On the back of their time cards, they would list the parts from the parts room they had used for that aircraft. That was all the information available. From that data an invoice was generated. It was like being a detective in a high-profile crime scene. I loved it. In three months Sam's shop billing was up to date. Sam had other projects for me to do, but some things had developed that I needed to consider.

When we moved to Texas back in 1979, I had studied for and passed the real estate broker's exam for the State of Texas. Since I still held an active real estate license I called Don and Karen Maloney, who owned a real estate agency, to see if they could use another agent. We met at their office on Sunday afternoon. It was they, not me, who brought up the subject of whether or not I needed to wear my artificial legs. They just didn't care if I were short or tall. I could wear the legs or not wear them. They wanted me to be comfortable. It was not an issue to them. It was my decision. Their open willingness to hire me, short or tall, surprised me.

What was going on? Only last evening I was visiting with my friend Glenda. Sitting on the floor playing cards, I needed to go to the bathroom. With the artificial legs on, the effort to stand up was considerable.

Glenda casually remarked, "Why do you keep wearing those heavy legs? You don't need to wear them."

Instantly I was angry and defensive. "I have to wear them," I said sharply. Glenda recognized she had touched a nerve, smiled and dropped the subject.

But maybe I didn't have to wear them. I was fully functional without them. In fact, I was much more agile and mobile without them. I had worn them for 32 years. I had never considered *not* wearing them. They were part of my daily routine. I had put my legs on each morning just as others put on their shoes or panty hose. I loved this tall world where I could see others at eye level. I loved coordinating the clothes, shoes and blazers. I felt like I looked good when I marched off to work. I was 51 years old. Was the price in energy and mobility I paid to function in the legs becoming too high?

One of my justifications for wearing them had fallen apart when Don and Karen hired me to sell real estate for them, with or without the legs. I had wondered if I would be hired for *any* position as a short person. Obviously my height was not a big deal. They were only interested in my performance as an agent. I could certainly move about much more easily without the ten pounds laced on each leg. Steps were difficult. Carrying anything took precision and balance. So what was it that tied me to them, day after day? Ego? Vanity? Pride? What will people think? And finally the basic human need to fit in and feel a part of Life. Did I need the aid of wood and metal laced to my legs to feel a part of Life? Had I deluded myself that the only way I could feel okay was to attach those heavy prostheses to my tiny body? This sounded pretty insane to me. It seemed madness to think I needed to punish my body with this needless, strenuous pursuit any longer. Of course there wasn't any God to help me sort it out.

Dr. Bob Gibson, a Master Teacher and at one time a practicing psychiatrist, was a regular guest speaker at the chapel. As my mentor, he had told me, "Donna, people don't care if you're short or tall. They love you anyway. And remember, we can all deal with 'what is.'"

"What is?" I was jarred, remembering that conversation. "What is?" Of course. For 32 years I had been trying to change "what is" into "what I thought it ought to be." I was short. I was embarrassed to be short. Being tall like other people removed most of my discomfort. I was at a turning point. Which way held the least discomfort: to be tall, safe, yet physically stressed or to be short and emotionally uncomfortable? It was time to do what was to my advantage, regardless of the pain and clamoring ego.

Okay, I told myself. I'll just go to the real estate office short. For everything else I'll be tall. That sounded reasonable. Deep down I knew that sooner or later I would have to set the legs aside. I might as well get it over with. The decision was made. I would start my new job at Maloney Realty the following day – short.

I had no idea, fortunately, what challenges lay before me.

CHAPTER 26

Fear, guilt, anger, inferiority
and insecurity are illusions.
Man was never designed to have them.

The night was restless. Fear seemed to cling to me like a shroud. I was surprised. It sounded simple enough. Just walk out of the house in the morning without those heavy legs, climb easily into the car, and drive handily to work. I was shocked by the intensity of the fear that immobilized me. What made this simple transition such a big deal?

Morning finally came. My wardrobe was tailored to clothe the towering five-foot-eight-inch gal. What could I wear? It was early November and I would need a jacket. Did I have any jackets or sweaters short enough to not drag the floor? I found a green pullover V-necked sweater. Around the house I had been wearing a pair of green plaid pants I had cut off from longer ones. These would match the sweater. And finally, I added a pair of moccasins for my size-one feet.

Even though the fear was still there, I never considered throwing in the towel. At any moment I could lace on the tall legs and call the whole thing off. The decision I had made to face this transition was deep and strong enough to be in charge, regardless of what my emotions were doing. I put one foot in front of the other and walked to the car. Perspiration oozed from every pore of my body. I felt naked, vulnerable, paranoid, insecure and scared.

I opened the door to the real estate office. Most of my co-workers had never seen me short. Their surprise was obvious. Just as 32 years before everyone was shocked to see me 20 inches taller, they now were seeing me 20 inches shorter. They couldn't help responding with shock and surprise. The change was radical.

There was another difference. Thirty-two years ago the experience of suddenly being five feet eight inches was exhilarating. The excitement and fun of being tall neutralized all the hardships and difficulties. Now, I did not want to be short. But, I also knew that the time had come to set the legs aside and not be tall anymore. The inner conflict was overwhelming. As a result of all this conflict, I ended up having the worst cold I could ever remember.

By noon things were a bit easier. All of the agents climbed into Don's wagon to drive around and look at new listings. My fellow agents didn't know whether to lift me into the wagon, offer to help or just watch as I lifted myself onto the seat. This different me was a new experience for all of us.

The freedom of mobility was starting to sink in. How easy it was to step up on a curb or climb stairs or jump into a car or run into the store without dragging 20 inches and 20 pounds along with me. This did, indeed, make the physical effort to function incredibly easier.

But my ego was not going to let me off the hook easily. It was not ready to give up the idea that the tall legs made me feel okay about myself. I felt as if pain oozed from every cell of my body. Many nights I woke up and the sheets would be soaked with my perspiration. I wondered if I was losing my mind.

I called Dr. Bob for some guidance. He told me, "Donna, you're playing roles. If you're short, play the role of a short person to the hilt. When you're tall, play the tall role to the hilt. Don't make the change too quickly. It could be harmful to you."

That sounded reasonable. I would sell real estate six days a week and play the short role. Each Wednesday I drove to the Cleburne Municipal Airport to do Sam's shop billing. On that day I laced on my legs and played the tall role. Betty and Sam didn't know until the next April that I was short the other six days of the week. I felt like two different people. Maybe I'm schizophrenic, I thought.

This was not working very well. Everything seemed hopeless. I looked in the closet for something to wear – and burst into tears. If I was going to stick with this decision to be short I had better alter some clothes to wear. I selected four pair of slacks, cut off 20 inches and began hemming them up. Trips to the clothing stores only deepened the despair. I would walk through the racks of beautiful clothes, then run to the fitting room and weep.

On the way home one evening, the despair was overwhelming. I stopped by to see Tanya, my best friend. I pulled into the driveway, but couldn't get out of the car.

Tanya came out and sat in the car, holding me while I cried. Then she said, "Donna, with your artificial legs on, you're handicapped. With your legs off, you're exceptional."

Those precious words continued to give me strength and encouragement in the gloomy and difficult days ahead.

Attending the office Christmas party was as unthinkable as climbing Mt. Everest.

Clothes were the big objection, although this was only a cover-up for my feelings of not being "okay." Tanya's husband was a fellow agent and they would be going to the party. Tanya reassured me, "Donna, this is the perfect time to step out socially. You'll be with all the people who love and support you." At that moment, I said, "Okay, I'm going." In the next moment, "No, I can't do it." The resistance was intense. There were no pretty clothes to wear and appropriate shoes for my little feet were impossible. I could have worn my legs and been tall, but I didn't want to do that, either.

The evening turned out to be delightful. No one cared whether I was short or tall. I could easily see all of the turmoil was within me. It had nothing to do with anyone else. I alone was responsible for how I perceived things. I could continue in this pitiful, hardheaded, stubborn, ego-driven mood or I could drop it. No one or no thing was causing me to be miserable or depressed. All of the powerful resistance to this dynamic change arose within me. My ego didn't want me to change. It deliberately sucked me into making clothes, shoes, appearance, what others think, and comfort zones important. It was all ego stuff. Was I going to let the ego run my life, or was I ready to step out of that mind set into freedom? The choice was mine. Bondage or slavery?

One of my tender spots was my self-consciousness about my physical appearance. This attitude was self-defeating and non-productive. In an attempt to consciously overcome this self-centeredness, I contacted the local Avon lady about becoming a representative. A territory was open near my house. Armed with the sample kit and order pad I proceeded to become acquainted with my neighbors.

Good intentions were easy. Actions were more difficult. I would lie on the couch after supper, dreading making the calls. In order to pry myself off the couch, I made a pact that I only had to make three calls a night and reminded myself that in one hour it would all be over. The resistance was heavy. I crawled out of the house, into the car and down the street – without letting the mind and all its tricks control me. I found everyone friendly. Many were lonely and welcomed someone to visit with. They usually bought something so I would come back to see them when their order arrived. This wonderful response from others was refreshing and uplifting. It neutralized some of that negative energy that seemed intent on destroying me.

Thinking myself into the feeling I wanted would not work. I could choose how I wanted to feel, but I could not use this same destructive mindset to produce that feeling. I had to *act* myself into that feeling. That is why the Avon adventure was so valuable to me. Lying on the couch depressed changed nothing. Action held the magic power.

Some adjustments had to be made at work. As a real estate agent I talked to clients at my desk before taking them on a property tour. I discovered that if they didn't know I was short (which they couldn't know when I sat behind my desk) they would be surprised when I jumped down out of my chair. It was much easier for everyone if I greeted my clients at the door of my office, introduced myself and asked them to have a seat. This gave them a few minutes to adjust to my height and I didn't loose their attention as potential buyers when I slid out of my chair later.

Then something happened that refocused the whole picture.

CHAPTER 27

A human being is a point of awareness.

The February evening was warm, warm enough to sit on the deck overlooking the lake and watch the sunset. I tried to keep my mind on something interesting or on some distraction to avoid the mental turmoil that continued to attack me. In periods of silence, the same old questions bubbled up, none of which seemed to have an answer. This time it was somehow different. The brown wren was bellowing out its magnificent melody. Suddenly, I heard it. Really heard it. "What is it in me that takes those musical vibrations and transforms them into meaning and beauty?" I asked. "There's no sound until they hit my ears."

I then saw the sunset with its array of gold, pink and lavender.

Again I asked, "What is it in me that takes those color vibrations and changes the vibration into beauty and elegance?" In that moment I knew there was Something invisible and intangible in me that "lived me." There were no words to describe this Essence. This awareness or consciousness could not be reached by the finite mind. There were no courses to take, books to read, seminars to attend, tapes to listen to that could connect me to this unbelievable Reality. It could only be sensed when I was clear enough to discern it.

As a child I would ask myself, "Who am I? What is this 'I' that lives in this town, this country, lives in this house? Who in the hell am I?" There were no answers then.

I felt that now something had been revealed to me that I had been searching for all of my life. For the first time ever I knew who I was. I am an expression of the Infinite. That Infinite Presence in me does all the work. It walks me, talks me, makes my skin warm, makes my heart beat, makes my lungs breathe, makes my eyes see and my ears hear. If the Presence is removed from me, the body immediately begins to rot.

The Presence could be called by many names: God, Life, Essence, Spirit, Allah, Jesus, Buddha, Intelligence, Love. It really didn't matter. The only thing that mattered was that I acknowledged that it "lived me," that this Essence had been implanted in me and did all the work. One book I read said, "It is not I, but the Father within who doeth all the work." Also, I could not be separated from it. The book went on to say, "The Father and I are one." Oneness, not duality. I didn't know what all of this would mean, but there was a definite shift in the value I placed on my existence. I was so much more than I thought I was – it boggled my mind. If I were more, so also was everyone else.

I sat there a long, long time, feeling the warmth of my skin. I listened to my breathing and my heart beating. From that moment on there was no more doubt. I didn't need to know any more. I was at peace with the fact of my existence. There was no longer any urge to change anything or anybody, including myself. The Creative Spirit was far more intelligent that I was. I could wholeheartedly embrace Life on Life's terms.

Life now took on a different texture. The conflict and resistance to every "what is" was gone. I knew that I was on a journey of some sort and that this Partner loved me so much that It would bring into my experience everything I needed to evolve me and grow me into Oneness. It was as if this Partner, called Life, designed my every encounter and every experience and stamped on it: "Especially designed for Donna Lancaster."

I wish I could say that I remember all of the above 100 percent of the time, but I do not. I have times when I'm impatient and testy. I don't like what is going on and complain and whine. But the feeling of peace always returns when I am conscious enough to remember.

CHAPTER 28

There is no need to defend or justify anything.

In the winter of 1983 I received a call from some friends in Dallas. They had heard about a new airfreight company just starting up and it was going to hire only women pilots. If I was interested, they had a phone number to call for more information.

I wasted no time. I called immediately and asked them to send me an application, which they did. When I dropped the application into the mail I thought, "Wouldn't it be great to have a job doing what I love to do most – flying an airplane?"

In a few weeks, the company called to set up an interview.

Now came the big question. Should I go to the interview short or tall? I was at a turning point. Short or tall? I decided it would probably be to my advantage to be tall. After all, this was a big event and an opportunity of a lifetime. I wanted to make the most of it and put my best foot forward, which would be my wooden foot. Since I still didn't have any satisfactory clothes to wear, I could at least dress appropriately with the legs on.

I gathered up my log books and FAA certificates and headed for Love Field Airport in Dallas.

Everyone was very warm and friendly. They had four Piper Malibus on order. These were single engine planes with a healthy payload. We would be flying freight, mostly at night and in all kinds of weather. Most of the interview was about what they were planning and not about me at all. They said they would call.

Weeks went by. I continued to sell real estate – short, and work at Sam's on Wednesdays – tall. In February, Lightning Express called for me to come for another interview.

By this time I was more comfortable without the artificial legs.

"Shall I go to the interview short or tall?" I questioned. If they hired me, they would know I was short, anyway. I might as well face it now, rather than later.

A classy friend, Fran Hillen, was visiting me from Midland that week. On the morning of the interview we spent time arranging the new red skirt and matching blouse under a short jacket, along with a small over-the-shoulder bag. Shoes were still a problem for my small feet, so I had to make do with my moccasins. All in all, I looked rather good. Not like other people, but with what I had to work with, I looked decent.

I was a bit anxious on the drive to Dallas. "I guess if they don't want someone my size flying their planes, now is a good time to settle the issue."

There was one problem with wearing a skirt. A long stairway led to the executive offices. If there were anyone behind me, they could see right up my little short dress. I waited until the stairway was clear, then dashed up the steps.

The interview went well. They hired me. The fact that I had dissolved from five foot eight inches to three foot ten inches was never mentioned, perhaps not even noticed. They couldn't have cared less.

The chief pilot, Marilyn, and another pilot and I all went out to lunch. The restaurant chosen was Celebration where all of the executives went for lunch. I was relieved and excited. I wanted to be at my very best. This was truly a celebration. When the tasty meal was over, I tried to push my seat back so I could climb down out of the chair. However, the chair wouldn't push back. It pushed over and fell backward. I toppled over, bottom up and feet in the air. A hundred pair of startled eyes settled on my position on the floor. I leveled my gaze on Marilyn and smiled, saying, "Hell of a way to impress my new employer!"

Thank goodness we could all laugh hysterically about it.

Initially, I was to start on May 1, 1984. This was delayed a month until June 1. During May, Tanya and I spent a day in Dallas apartment hunting. We settled on the last place we looked at, not because it was anything special, but because it was the last place on the list. We were tired and it was a good as any. I would be the first tenant in #136 of the new apartment complex.

The kitchen was handy, with a large walk-in pantry. The large bedroom also had a walk-in closet, and the living room had patio doors, looking out on a small concrete, fenced area. I filled out the application and paid first and last months' rent. It was just beginning to dawn on me that I was moving to Dallas. There was a lot ahead of me. Rent the lake house. Have a garage sale. Pack. Decide what to do with Molly. Quit the three jobs I had. Leaving the lake, my friends, the comfort and ease of lake living was never an issue.

CHAPTER 29

Surrender:
Ceasing to think I know "what ought to be."

I found someone to rent the house furnished, which simplified the packing. The garage sale went well and I got rid of everything I wouldn't need. I was not sentimental over things and could trim my possessions down to the essentials. I would take the game table and chairs, the couch, a bed and chest, clothes, dishes – and my two pair of legs, just in case.

Molly, my delightful poodle, was not an easy decision. Molly was my companion, comforter and best friend. We had been through a lot together. I knew I would be flying and away from home. What was best for each of us? My next-door neighbor, Alma, helped with this touchy one. She asked me, "What has more value in your life? Molly or your new job?"

The answer was obvious. I would have to find Molly a good home. This was so painful I could hardly think about it. All of a sudden the same intense, guilty feelings I had had about Neal surfaced. When he died, I felt I had deserted him, my best friend. Now, faced with leaving Molly, these same feelings came rushing back. I started weeping and couldn't seem to stop. When it was finally over, I knew what I had to do. My friend, Lucille, had kept Molly from time to time when I had to leave town for a day or two. She would provide a wonderful, loving home for her.

Tanya's husband had a pickup and three other friends wanted to help move me. On Thursday, May 31, they loaded up the truck and headed for Dallas. It was late in the afternoon before they had transferred everything from the truck into my apartment. They left me, cheerfully waving and calling, "Have fun. Lots of luck."

After settling in I realized I needed some groceries to begin my new life, I drove to the store and picked up milk, eggs and bread. On the way home a boy ran a stoplight and smashed into my car.

My first thought was not, "Is anybody hurt?" but "How can I get to work on Monday without a car to drive? I can't drive just anybody's car. I have to have hand-controls."

The police finally came. The boy was given a ticket, and, of course, didn't have any insurance. The officer asked me what wrecker service and repair place I wanted to use.

"I have no idea. I've lived in Dallas only one hour. Can you help me?"

He was very gracious and called a wrecking service at the Buick auto shop to tow my car away. He loaded me and my groceries, covered with slimy broken eggs, into his police cruiser, and drove me to my new apartment.

This was not what I had in mind. No phone. No car. Nothing could be done until morning. So I started unpacking boxes. This kept me from creating numerous scary scenarios, all of which were illusions and a waste of energy. By midnight I was unpacked and exhausted. I fell asleep instantly.

Since my phone would not be connected until later in the day, I used the phone in the apartment's business office. My first call was to the insurance company. The information that they had for me was fantastic. Avis would put hand controls on cars. Eureka! That was a tremendous help. My greatest concern was transportation. My apartment was 13 miles from Love Field. A car was not a luxury, but a necessity. I called Avis at DFW Airport. They would have a car ready for me by 2:00 p.m. I couldn't have been more pleased and excited. All of the other situations I would have to deal with amounted to nothing at all. I had a car I could drive. Everything would work out.

Well, so I thought until Monday morning.

CHAPTER 30

Life is the Teacher.

The freight company had hired about 20 female pilots for their operation. We gathered in the executive office to receive our initial briefing. We were all excited about the opportunity to do what we loved most and get paid for it – fly. The CEO came into the room, rather soberly.

Her first comment was, "I have some distressing news. The finances for this operation have been withdrawn. We are no longer in business."

The silence could have been cut with a knife. Some of the pilots had moved to Dallas from other states. They had quit jobs, left their friends or family, given their pets away and made major sacrifices and adjustments, just as I had done. They were stunned, then angry. Watching the groups of women complain and whine about their situation, I knew whining was not the answer. My mother had taught me that little gem 40 years ago when I whined about washing the dishes. I didn't know what I'd do. Maybe the Ramada would hire me as a maid. I was just the right height and was a whiz at making beds. I had to get out of this office, before I got pulled into the self-defeating and complaining energy that was toxic.

Just as I started out the door, Marilyn, the chief pilot, approached me.

"Donna, I understand Jet East is looking for an aircraft dispatcher. You might want to check it out."

"Aircraft dispatcher? Well, it might be better than cleaning rooms at the Ramada. Thanks for the tip."

Aircraft dispatcher? I had no idea what that meant. It must have something to do with airplanes and that always captured my attention. If I had been asked to write down a hundred things I would be interested in, aircraft dispatcher would not have been on the list. I was glad I had discarded goal setting years ago. I found it was much too stressful. If my mind had been set on a pilot job, I might have missed this opportunity of a lifetime. So I marched to Jet East, resumé in hand, and asked to see the chief pilot. Ched Bart, the chief pilot, was standing at the door of the break room. Evidently some of the other pilots who had been hired and were now jobless had already been to Jet East looking for a job. He was cool and unfriendly. He did not ask me to come to his office or sit down. I stood there, looking up at him, ill at ease.

"I understand you're looking for a dispatcher. I want to apply for the job." I offered. "Here's my resume."

We both remained standing. Ched began reading the resume. Silence. Finally, he suggested we sit on the couch in the waiting room and talk.

Jet East was a full service, aircraft fixed-base operator. They provided fuel, aircraft maintenance, avionics, aircraft interiors and an impressive fleet of corporate aircraft for charter. At the time the fleet consisted of six Lear Jet 35s, three Lear Jet 25s, One Challenger, two King Airs, one Falcon 20 and a Citation III. Forty Pilots were needed to crew these planes.

The personnel in charter sales took phone calls for those wanting to charter a plane. Then a plane was selected and a crew was briefed. This all sounded simple. But the amount of information necessary to handle this was overwhelming. This included knowing which pilots could fly which aircraft. Some of this data also included distance of flight, time of flight, fuel consumption, runway lengths, hours of airport operations all over the country, airport restrictions, customs, catering … and especially, how the client was going to pay for the trip. A flight from Love Field to Los Angeles and back in a Lear Jet was over $8,000. I sat spellbound as Ched explained all of this to me.

Finally, he asked, "Would you be available to talk with the Director of Operations and the President of Jet East tomorrow?"

I had nothing else to do. "Of course." I answered.

The interviews the next day went well. They wanted me to start to work the next morning. Salary was not discussed. I didn't care what it was and didn't bring up the subject. I was just thankful to have a job.

The dispatch room was called the nerve center of Jet East. One entire wall, over 20 feet, was one huge blackboard. The days were at the top, covering two weeks of future charter trips. Along the left side of the board were all the different aircraft. Each block was filled in with the information regarding that particular flight: Destination, departure times, catering, crew, number of passengers, crew briefings. Each piece of information had to be confirmed on the day preceding the flight.

Ched reminded me that we were dealing with very wealthy clients. Mistakes would not be tolerated. "If I don't do this the way you want me to, let me know. I'm a big girl and I can take it," I said confidently.

Those words would come back to haunt me.

CHAPTER 31

Whenever we make anything important,
we are anxious.

For a few days I sat and watched the activity in the dispatch room. It was overwhelming. All the pilots looked alike. I didn't know a King Air from a Lear Jet. I had none of the information that seemed to be required to just answer the telephone, which was always ringing. I left work each evening dazed and exhausted. Self-doubt gnawed at me. "Maybe I'm not bright enough to learn this." I sensed their expectations, as well as mine, far exceeded my capacity to absorb all I needed to know.

At the end of the month, Ched called me into his office. "We're going to see how big a girl you are."

I sat there silently as Ched enumerated all the things I had been doing wrong. Some were true. Some were not. He informed me I would be re-evaluated in two weeks. If things hadn't changed by then, they would have to replace me. The significance of his words ignited every cell of my body. Here I was, 52 years old, and I had found the job of a lifetime. I wanted to learn to do it so much that any other option was unthinkable.

When he finished, I said quietly, "Thank you for talking to me. I'll redouble my efforts and do the best I can."

When I climbed into the rental car I was driving, I burst into tears.

"This is the most wonderful job I've ever had. By God, I'm going to do this if it kills me."

It nearly did.

I began taking books and schedules home at night to memorize. I memorized the aircraft tail numbers and matched them with who could fly them. I studied FAA regulations concerning charter operations and what we could do or not do. I screamed in the car on the way to work. Fear almost paralyzed me. When the tension in the dispatch room was high, I went to the bathroom and did deep breathing exercises.

For several weeks I had had an intense pain in my back. I thought I had pulled a muscle. At night, unable to sleep, I took hot baths, used ice packs, tried to watch TV, or drove to the grocery store, which was open all night. I sat in the middle of the bed reciting poetry or the Twenty-third Psalm. I was taking four aspirin and four extra-strength Tylenol every two hours. Lack of sleep was taking its toll.

After two weeks of this nightmare, I told Ched on Friday, "I have a doctor's appointment this afternoon. I need to leave a little early."

I drove to the Lake to see Wesley, Tanya's husband, my friend and chiropractor. I told him what was happening. Wesley told me, "Donna, you have shingles."

"No, I can't have shingles," I sobbed.

"You have a very stressful job. I suggest you quit. We can treat the shingles, but if you continue to be under stress, there will be another physical adaptation."

"Wesley, I can't quit. This is the most wonderful job I've ever had. Tell me what I can do to stay in the job and not let it make me sick."

He had no answer.

The renters at my lake house had moved out and I could stay there over the weekend. I had a prescription for pain pills filled and spent the weekend in bed. By Sunday afternoon I felt much better and returned to Dallas.

I didn't take any medicine while I was working. The atmosphere in the dispatch room was so intense I felt no pain at work. This was a wonderful lesson for me. Intense pain could be handled by shifting my mind to something so riveting that pain would not be sensed.

The two weeks probation had passed and Ched had said nothing to me. I was not going to bring up the subject because I didn't want to know. It was easier to live in the unknown than to face failure. I just did the best I knew how. I could at least operate the computers and give quotes to those who called. The people were starting to have names I could remember. The flip charts I had made were helping me tie things together. I had to memorize the planes, their "N" or registration numbers, who owned them, the owners' secretaries' names and what kind of liquor they wanted on board.

The pilots couldn't have been nicer. They were a delightful group of young men who loved to fly more than anything else, just like me. At Jet East they could build up their hours and go on to the major airlines. Jet East was a classy place and hired a classy group of pilots. I loved them all.

It took one year of learning before I felt comfortable in dispatch. If I didn't have the answer, at least I knew where to find it. I was always ready to go to work and the issue with Ched was never mentioned.

Years later when he left Jet East for another job, I told him, "Ched, I want to thank you for what you did for me. You forced me to dig in and do it. You pulled the very best out of me. That was a great gift."

CHAPTER 32

A conscious person has reverence for all life …
and that includes even mosquitoes.

There were a few bright spots in those stressful days at Jet East. I hadn't lived in Dallas very long when Tanya called one evening to see how I was getting along. "What are you doing?" she asked.

"I'm sitting here reading the phone book." I replied cheerfully.

"Reading the phone book? Have you gone mad?" With millions of listings in the Dallas area, this seemed rather pointless. She proceeded with caution. "What is that all about?"

"Well, I didn't make it to the library before it closed. So I picked up the phone book. You'd be amazed at the plethora of information they put in it: schools, civic events, maps, points of interest, etc. It's fascinating reading. I thought I would get acquainted with this city I'm living in. Besides it's much more interesting than anything I can find on TV."

It sounded so funny we started laughing hysterically.

Another bright spot in my new life was Harrison. I wanted a bit of companionship in my apartment so I accepted a baby finch from friends who had just had a crop of them. I named him Harrison, my grandfather's middle name. He wore the name proudly.

Harrison Lancaster was about four inches long with a circle of orange on each cheek, a bright red beak and a voice that carried for blocks. He was full of conversation, most of it meaningless chatter. His hearing was acute and he had much to say about any insignificant noise. He brightened the house with his squeaky early morning songs. He was also my teacher.

For instance, the time had come for Harrison to have a new cage. The old one was rusty and had droppings all over it. The new cage was a bit larger and arranged differently. The food cup was in a different place. The round perches were stretched inside the cage at different angles. A new bathing tub was installed. A new swing hung from the top of the cage. Naturally, he was scared and didn't want to be touched. He flew frantically around in his old cage for several minutes before I could hold him long enough to put him in his new cage.

For the first 12 hours he sat in a corner and pouted. He did not like the new cage. He wanted his old, familiar, comfortable one where everything was convenient. The new swing threatened him and the new perches required risky flights to reach. Out of necessity he found his food and water. He would not venture any farther from his safe corner. After 24 hours he could hit three perches in his circle around the cage, briefly touching his new swing on the way. It took him three days to conquer his favorite perch, his swing. He was teaching me that change is an adjustment and a process. Accept the uncomfortable for a while. It will pass.

At this point I needed the lesson. My uncomfortable level was off the charts. Negativity had convinced me that it would never be any different. Watching Harrison gave me the comfort of knowing, "This too, will pass." And it did.

The time came for Harrison to have a female roommate; her name was Harriet. Harriet seemed crazy about him, so they set up housekeeping. With a bit of encouragement, such as putting nesting material and a bamboo nest in the cage, Harrison and Harriet proceeded to start a family. They padded the entire inside of the nest with cotton. Harriet laid three eggs the size of M&M's. They took turns sitting on them. Each day they turned the eggs over to keep the delicate membrane on the inside of the shell from sticking to it. In 12 days the eggs hatched. For the next 12 days the tiny birds were fed and watered by their attentive parents who patiently filled each tiny beak with nestling food and water. When the three birds (two boys and one girl) emerged from the nest, they were nearly the size of their parents.

Neither Harriet nor Harrison had ever taken a parenting course or read a book on *How to Raise Baby Finch*. Innately they had all the information they needed. Although they had no self-awareness, the techniques for survival operated effortlessly. They did not complain or blame. They did not argue about who was going to feed the kids in the middle of the night or blame each other because we have all these mouths to feed. They did not worry about whether they were doing it right. They just did it. The Life Force within each of them knew how to do it all.

Observing them reminded me that Life, the Essence within me, was totally wise and contained everything I needed for each encounter, for each moment. I had made it extremely important to make it at Jet East, leaving me exhausted, fearful and anxious. The Truth was, "Nothing is important." The world was doing fine before I got here and would do fine after I left the planet. So, how important am I in this wisp of time? If they fired me, so what? Life would go on. Harrison and Harriet lived in the present moment, doing what was before them to do, without worry or anxiety. If their babies died, they would feel no guilt or regret. They had given their best. Could I do likewise? Absolutely!

Knowing the Truth does set us free.

Part of the mating ritual involved Harrison pecking Harriet's neck. He was so persistent she developed bleeding wounds that wouldn't heal. I had to put them in separate cages. When Harrison objected to this arrangement, I explained to him that due to his aggressiveness, it was his own fault he was living alone. Sadly, Harriet died of her wounds. Harrison lived to be 14 years old, which is a very long life for a finch. He had enriched my life beyond measure.

CHAPTER 33

We live in that which we radiate.

In 1989 I moved from the apartment to a prestigious 32-story high-rise, only five miles from Love Field. I had friends living in the Preston Tower who had invited me to their apartment several times. The skyline from their windows was fabulous.

"I wonder if I can afford to live here? This really suits my style!" I dreamed. At the urging of my friends, I contacted the leasing agent.

"Do you have any units for lease?" I asked.

They did. I made arrangements to look at several. The first one I saw was just perfect. On the eighth floor the view was outstanding. The floor-to-ceiling windows faced south from the living room and bedroom. Patio doors opened from each room onto a 5-foot-by-35-foot balcony. There were lots of closets, thick plush carpets, eight-foot ceilings, instant hot water from the hot water faucet, and self-cleaning oven. The building offered valet service, underground parking and exquisite décor. The package became more appealing when I discovered Wednesday night bridge games. I decided to take the risk for one year. If I had any trouble making the monthly payments, by the end of the year, I would move. Meanwhile I would embrace high-rise living to the fullest.

Tanya came up from the lake to help me pack, move and arrange my new home. Tanya, my best friend, had always been there for me even though many of the times had been painful and miserable. This time it was different. There was joy and fun and laughter. During the packing she would ask: "Do you need this? Do you use this?"

If the answers were no, it went in the trash. No argument. Out it went. We both laughed hysterically. With Tanya's knack for decorating and my checkbook, the new apartment was fit for a princess. I truly felt like one.

One of the ladies I played bridge with asked me one afternoon, "Do you know of anyone who would like a part-time job with the oil company on the second floor?"

At this time I was working nights at Jet East. I went to work at 4:00 p.m., left Jet East at midnight, or when I finished the work. If there were charter calls during the night, the calls were patched through to me at home. Some nights I might have several calls and maybe a flight or two to set up. Southwest Organ Bank used Jet East Lear Jets to pick up hearts, livers and lungs from all over the country. These flights were usually done at night, because that was when the operating room facilities at the hospitals were available. The donating patients were on life support until the Southwest Organ Bank team of nurses and doctors came for the organs. As dispatcher, I made all the arrangements for these flights. I went off call at 8:00 a.m., so I had the morning and most of the afternoon free. A part-time job was just what I needed to fill those empty hours.

I had an interview with Charles Harding and his son Rick, owners of the oil company. Here I was again with those old conditioned ideas pulling at me. "Will they hire someone as short as I am?" I didn't need to worry. I started to work as Mr. Harding's secretary the next morning at 9:00.

I again faced another learning curve. I had had a very impressive and painful learning experience eight years before when I started with Jet East. I had learned the lesson well. This time I was gentler with myself and learned what I could, one day at a time. I refused to make anything important, instead enjoying the work, even if I couldn't do it perfectly the first time. Charlie was a superb and patient teacher. He complimented me when I got it right and gently nudged me to do it over when my work fell short. And best of all, taking the elevator from the eighth floor to the second floor took me only a minute to get to work.

Life was fun.

CHAPTER 34

Life is a series of events,
all of which will pass.

In 1995 Jet East was sold to a competitor. I was faced with several options. I could stay on at Jet East, essentially as a new hire; I could go to another charter company; or I could move back to the lake. It really didn't matter. I knew I would be okay no matter what I was doing or where I was living. I was 63 years old. Maybe it was time to quit this work, work, work. I applied at several charter operators and had an interview with one. I set a salary in my head that I would need in order to stay in Dallas and let the chips fall where they may. By the end of June I knew I would go back to the lake.

Tanya and Wesley helped me move home. Harrison rode in his cage on the front seat. It didn't take him long to learn how to balance his weight so he wouldn't fall off his perch when the car turned a corner. The temperature was 103 degrees when we finished packing the U-Haul truck and headed for Whitney. I sensed the door slowly closing on the wonderful life and jobs and friends I had in Dallas. I knew this new phase would be just as wonderful and fun as I allowed it to be.

When we arrived at the house, my thoughtful bridge friends had left sandwiches, salad and cookies on the bar, knowing that all of us would be hot and tired when we got in.

There was work and cleaning to be done on the house. I had the entire inside painted white along with new white carpet and drapes. I hired some of the work done. A lot of it, such as papering, caulking, cleaning windows, I did myself, provided it didn't interfere with a bridge game.

CHAPTER 35

Aging is a chronic disorder.

One of the greatest challenges I face is dealing with the aging process. Most of my life I have been able to adapt and function with very few physical limitations. Now my body is changing. The skin is losing its tone. Wrinkles silently emerge here and there. My energy level is different. I don't want to admit that my body is slowly but surely disintegrating. I have always had good health. Illness was foreign and repulsive. I know anger, boredom, anxiety, fear, resentment, depression and all the negative emotions produce chemicals that the body is not equipped to handle. The body, therefore, has to adapt to these toxic emotions. This adaptation is called illness. To stay healthy I have to be free of these destructive states. I have done this to the best of my ability. For the most part, my inner state has been upbeat and enthusiastic. Yet the disintegration of the body continues.

Some of my friends were investing in face lifts and tummy tucks. After thinking about it for over a year, I decided to check it out. I called for an appointment with a plastic surgeon in Waco. The receptionist said that an evaluation would be $80.

"That's all right. When do you have an appointment?"

A date was set. I took a bath and began dressing for the interview. I had been wearing some black socks around the house which were covered with white paint. They fit perfectly in my boots, so I wore them. The doctor was only going to look at my face, anyway. I also needed to shave my legs, but who would see them? Off I went to Waco. When I jumped up on the examining table the plastic surgeon pointed at my legs and asked, "How did this happen?"

"I have a congenital deformity. There are no knee joints. No tibia or fibula. No hip joints, only muscle and tissue. I have no ball and socket connecting the pelvis and femur." I explained.

"Do you mind if I take a look?"

Dirty socks. Hairy legs. "Of course not," I offered.

He was fascinated from a physician's viewpoint.

He then evaluated my face. He suggested removing the puffiness from over and under the eyes.

"How much money are we talking about?" I asked. When I was given the cost, I said, "I'll think about it and let you know."

He guided me to the appointment desk and told his secretary, "Anytime Donna calls for her surgery, work her in."

The secretary told me to leave by a different door than the one I came in.

"But I haven't paid my bill." I protested.

"The doctor has marked your chart 'no charge' today."

The price of surgery was too high. Hadn't my life been about realizing that the outward form, the body, is only a house to live in? The real Essence, the real Being was encased in this miraculous instrument, the body. Changing the shape and looks of the face wouldn't change that Essence.

I remembered Harrison and the aging I saw him experience. He wasn't as active as he aged. He spent less time on his swing and more time taking naps. It took more energy for him to fly up to his perches. I had never heard him complain or whine about age. A face lift? It had never occurred to him. His attitude toward life was one of total acceptance. His little mind had not accumulated a lifetime of conditioned ideas about death and dying. This left him free to experience each day to the fullest. He had no preconceived ideas about how life ought to be. He probably had various aches and pains, which he took for granted. He would not let those irritations diminish his joy of living. He had not made the basic decision at his moment of birth as humans do that the whole purpose of living was to be comfortable. He had no ideals or illusions to live up to that would destroy his body. He was 14 years old when he died. He had taught me much about life.

I began looking for the things I could do. My total state of health involved only four aspects: activity, environment, nutrition and inner feeling. Activity? Shuffling cards exercised my fingers. That was about it. I bought the book, *Yoga for Dummies*, and worked for an hour each morning on the positions I could do. Yoga not only stretched the body, but it was also helpful in practicing present moment attention, which seemed to be all there is.

Even though push-ups were not a yoga routine, I did them regularly. A lot of my activities demanded I use my arms. It was vital to keep them strong. I lifted myself into the car, onto the commode, into a chair, up and down stairs. Each time I lifted my body, which was many times a day, I lifted 70 pounds. The hardest part was to keep interested in doing the exercises. The tricky mind would invent hundreds of reasons to justify skipping a day or two: I didn't have enough time; I didn't feel like it; it was too cold, or hot; missing one day wouldn't matter, etc. This inertia or resistance was self-defeating. I knew I would do only that which I valued. At this point I put great value on having a healthy body. But sometimes the resolve was not enough to drag me out of the chair onto the yoga pad. Yet I knew if I just did it, I would feel better physically. I would also feel better about myself.

I watched the ducks sitting on the lake. When they started to fly out of the water it took tremendous energy to break through the surface tension of the water. Once they were free of it, they soared effortlessly. They didn't sit there waiting for a better day when it would be easier or when they had more energy. They just pushed right through it.

Within the last few weeks I bought a Wii. This remarkable program that uses the TV and a DVD has changed my attitude toward exercise. I love to do the tennis, bowling, golf and baseball. I can stay interested and enthused about those games, which move me all over the living room. Wii has been a great help.

Nutrition? This area needed some attention. Food had never been one of my priorities. Hunger was not a driving force. I could eat or not eat. Eating cottage cheese from the container because it was quick and easy would have to change. Only I was responsible for my nutrition. I had to make a decision to provide my body with adequate fuel.

To learn more about this I went to the Optimum Health Institute in Austin for two weeks, where I learned to eat better. They suggested no cooked foods because enzymes are destroyed at 117 degrees. No sugar. No bread. No dairy products. No supplements. No caffeine. No meat. Although I didn't stay on such a strict diet, I did eat more raw fruits and vegetables. I avoided meat, bread and dairy products and sugar, most of the time. It was certainly a worthwhile education.

Environment? My physical environment couldn't have been nicer. My house overlooked Lake Whitney and the area was quiet and peaceful. I took a look at the energy I radiated around me and concluded that it was environmentally safe. My accumulation of plants, some 35 of them, was happy and healthy. That should tell me something.

Inner feelings? I knew negative emotions were destructive to my body. These emotions produced chemicals that were harmful to the body at a cellular level. I could check this out. I had noticed when I was upset, angry, or in a snit, that within 72 hours there would be a physical adaptation of some kind. I would have a headache, a rash, a runny nose, an upset stomach, a back ache or other irritations. When my attitude was one of peace and joy, the body would work quite harmoniously. I simply could not afford negative emotions.

Therefore, I simply could not afford to resist aging anymore. Resisting it would only speed up the process.

CHAPTER 36

All is well.

In addition to taking care of my body and emotions, I was learning how to nurture my spirit as well. A gift from the universe came to me that continues to give me lessons in growth daily. It all started when in 1979, Neal and I were still living in Siloam Spring, Arkansas. My friend Alma, in Whitney, called and invited me for a weekend seminar. She thought I would enjoy the speaker. I accepted and started making plans to go. It snowed all night on Thursday and there was no way the little plane and I could get off the runway. I stood at our back windows and realized that I had to go to Whitney. I told Neal, "I can't fly to Whitney, but I think I'll go anyway." I could drive the Suburban for the 450 mile trip.

Neal replied, "If you want to go that bad, then you had better go."

Nine hours later I pulled into Alma's driveway. When I walked into the house, Dr. Bob was cooking beans and cornbread for our supper. After we ate, we went to the chapel for his evening lecture. His words affected me like a spiritual shower bath. I couldn't believe my ears. I felt a sense of Truth and clarity that overwhelmed me. Maybe, just maybe, there was a way out of the morose and despair that had colored my life for years.

Dr. Bob Gibson became my mentor, my teacher until he died in 1994.

His remarkable Presence influenced, transformed and liberated thousands of us who knew him. He gave us *The Teachings*, a set of ideas for us to check out to see if they worked for us. These ideas have been gleaned from the many religious movements of the past thousands of years – The Tao, Buddhism, Christianity and others.

The Teachings and Dr. Bob's influence in my life are immeasurable. For the past 30 years they offered me the tools I needed to carve a life of peace and joy.

For instance, I now knew I was responsible for my inner state. No job or environment or situation could make me unhappy, or happy, unless I allowed it. I had seen that silly idea that if I was unhappy or upset something hadn't gone my way. Who was I to think that I would always have things my way? That was nonsense. That was insanity. Once I could see it, I could drop that misconception. I could also see that my purpose for living was to be comfortable. Unconsciously I had decided I deserved being comfortable. I wanted the right relationship, the right house, the right job, the right income, the right everything so I would be comfortable. So when discomfort came along, as it always did, I didn't like it. I would try to change it, ignore it, control it, blame someone for it, complain about it and generally be in a snit or in a state of conflict. I could see that this attitude was destructive. As long as I lived in this little precious body, there would always be some discomfort. That was the reality. Discomfort, or resistance to "what is," was a gift. Discomfort and resistance to "what is" were my Teachers. If I was resisting anything, I was operating from a misconception. Life had only one purpose for me – to evolve me into a conscious person. So the discomfort was a signal to me that I was operating from a misconception. Weed out the misconceptions, which were illusions based on expectations, and the conflict dissolved. My misconception had been that I had a right to be comfortable. As soon as I understood this, I was able to enthusiastically embrace resistance and discomfort. I was free to experience everything that came my way. Whether I liked it or not, had nothing to do with it. I was going to experience it anyway, so I might as well experience it gracefully. I didn't have to waste energy or time trying to arrange things to fit my idea of what life ought to be. I didn't have to wait for the ideal job or house or relationship to be okay. Life loved me so much that every encounter and every experience was tailored for my growth. Who was I to outguess the Creator? I had no idea "what ought to be" – for me or for others. What a relief it was that I no longer had to fix me or anybody else. As an experiencing entity I was here for the ride. I could fully and freely embrace whatever Life brought into my experience. "Resist nothing." The book said. Nothing needed to be changed. Everything was okay, just as it was. I was free to enjoy the ride.

CHAPTER 37

We are spiritual beings having a human experience.

The past few years have been wonderful. There have been a few bumpy places, but that is the way Life works. Evidently I needed those bumps to wake me up and teach me because the depth of the spiritual unfolding is limitless. The journey moves however it moves. I am not in charge. Krishnamurti once said, "I don't mind what happens to me." That seems to be a great place to be.

The beautifully carved artificial legs I wore for 32 years are now tucked snugly under the bed. Although it would take some practice, I could return to the tall world anytime. I hesitate to throw them away because they are irreplaceable. I even have some outdated clothes left over from my tall years.

Dr. Bob in his lectures recommended we ask ourselves four questions: What am I? Where am I? What is going on? And, what can I do? So, I am a privileged invited guest on this beautiful estate called Earth at an incredible Party put on by the Host, Life. This must be a Party. When there is a bunch of people together playing games it's called a Party. I arrived at the Party helpless, naked, toothless and unable to speak the language. I had two slaves to take care of me for 18 years. Ever since I arrived at the Party, the Host has provided me abundantly with everything I have needed. I have clothes to wear, a home to live in, a car to drive, food to eat, interesting things to do and interesting people to be around. I have it all. Why would I ever be afraid – afraid of sickness, death, pain, economic turmoil, discomfort? When I remember that I already have it all, I can live fearlessly. That is my intent.

Because I am so thankful to be invited to this incredible Party there might be something I could do to express my gratitude to the Host, (i.e. God, Life, Partner) for inviting me. I can do this by being considerate and harmless to the other guests, myself and the Planet. I also understand that I can make a contribution to Life by expressing a harmonious mood wherever I go. I'm not a hundred percent, but I do my best.

Perhaps in these troubled and violent times that may be the most valuable contribution I can make for all Mankind.

Keep the mood up ...
and don't make anything important.

EPILOGUE

The Assignment.

The manuscript was almost ready to be sent to the printer when some dramatic events occurred.

Three years ago the doctor said I had a leaky aortic valve in my heart. Since I had no symptoms, we ignored it. Several months ago I experienced considerable shortness of breath and went to a cardiologist to see what was going on. He said the faulty valve was probably due to a congenital deformity and I had lived with it all my life. Some tests were run and he recommended an aortic valve replacement. He said I would be in ICU for two days, rehab for ten days and then be on my merry way. This didn't sound too difficult, so I agreed to have the surgery.

This didn't work out like I had planned. During the 12 days I stayed in ICU many unexpected complications took place. I was clinically dead for six-and-a-half minutes, at which time I traveled the Universe for several days.

Tanya, my friend of 30 years, stayed faithfully by my side throughout the many procedures and knew that I had apparently died. Or did I? The following is what we pieced together about the incredible journey that happened to me.

Tanya called me about 9:30 on the morning on Tuesday, May 4 to let me know she was on her way to the hospital. When I answered the phone I said, "I'm back!" "From where?" She asked. "From Never, Never Land," I answered.

She jokingly asked if I'd seen Michael Jackson while I was there. I laughed and said, "No." I knew that I was back from wherever I had been since the morning of Friday, April 30 until Tuesday, May 4.

When Tanya arrived at the hospital I was sitting up in bed, alert and present. "What a trip! I've been in La La Land. I've been traveling the Universe." At this time no one had told me that I had *died* for a few minutes (according to the records) the previous Friday.

I called Tanya to my bedside, took her hand, wrapped both of my hands and arms around hers. I held her and began to softly weep. As I wept, I said, "There is a pool of consciousness. There is no heaven or hell. It is beautiful there." Tanya asked me, "Did you go there?" I replied by holding up my hand with my index finger and thumb slightly apart. "Last night I was on the edge. I was just on the cusp. It was so beautiful."

Tanya told me I had worked really hard to stay here and she felt I must have something more to do in life or I would have left this Planet. To this I began to weep. With great feeling, I replied, "I do have an assignment. I am to save people from the belief in Satan. There is no heaven or hell. No Satan – only a beautiful pool of consciousness."

Even as a little girl going to Sunday School at the Methodist Church, I couldn't buy the concept of heaven and hell. It just sounded like a control issue to me. I could never reconcile a God who loved me unconditionally with a God who judged my behavior and, if I didn't measure up, I would go to hell. These were diametrically opposing concepts which have been pounded into people for centuries. It may be a hard sell to convince people of this, however, since this is my assignment, I will give it my best shot!

There is no heaven or hell.
There is no Satan.

There is only a beautiful pool of consciousness.

Life is very, very good.
All is well.

Donna Lancaster
June 2010

ACKNOWLEDGEMENTS

My heartfelt thanks go to Tanya Sulak who has been my friend forever, through short and tall, and who has always believed in me. She knew when she could push me to write and wisely pulled back when I was stubborn, hardheaded and resisted writing another word. Her timely suggestions have greatly enhanced this book.

I wish to thank my brother Jack Hollingsworth, who has given me his solid support since the moment of my birth. He was always convinced that this book needed to be out there so others could experience this story.

Thanks to the remarkable men and women of Alcoholics Anonymous and Al-Anon. Their love, understanding and acceptance have enriched my life beyond measure.

I am deeply grateful to Melody Swan for bringing the story to life in book form.

I would like to thank my many, many friends who, to my surprise, never cared whether I was short or tall. Their support and encouragement were boundless.

Thank you, Life, for inviting me to the Planet for this magnificent journey.

LaVergne, TN USA
03 September 2010
195752LV00004B/7/P